Classic Cars Coloring Book

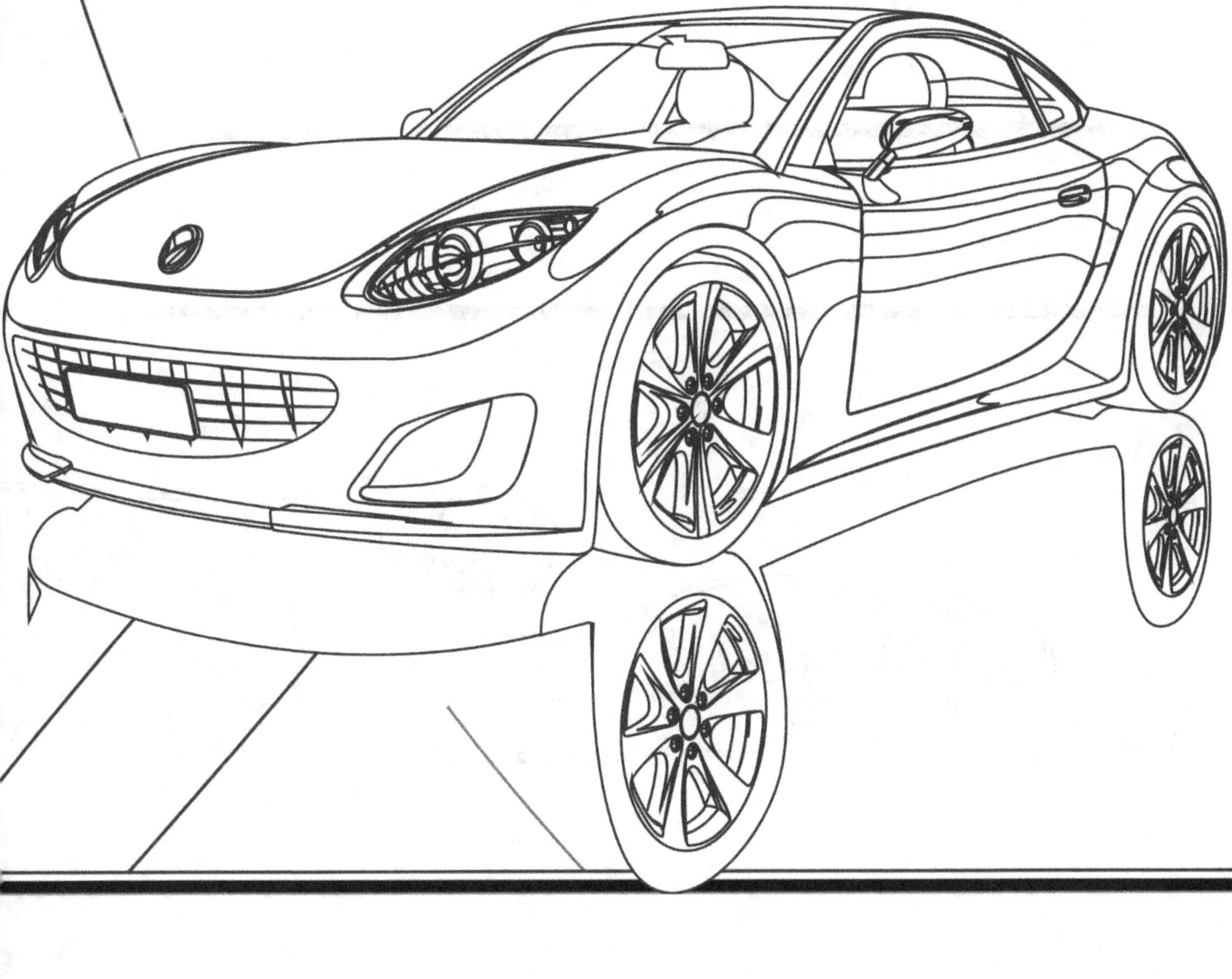

THIS BOOK BELONG TO

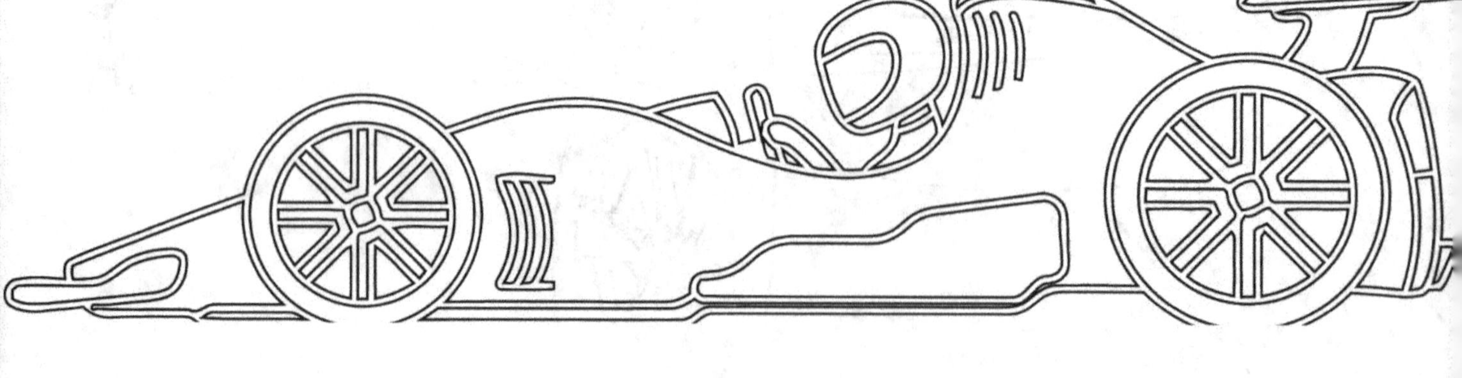

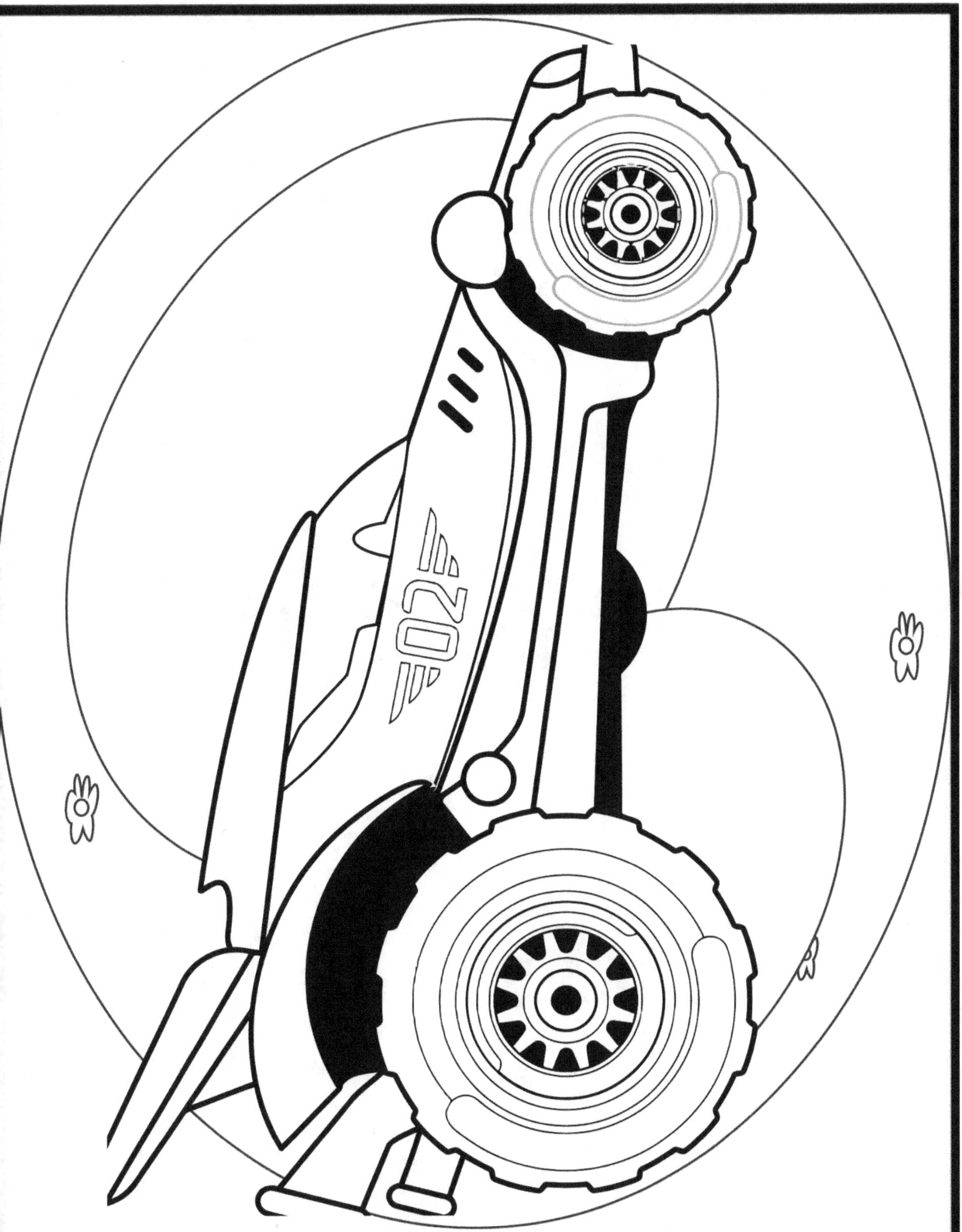
20

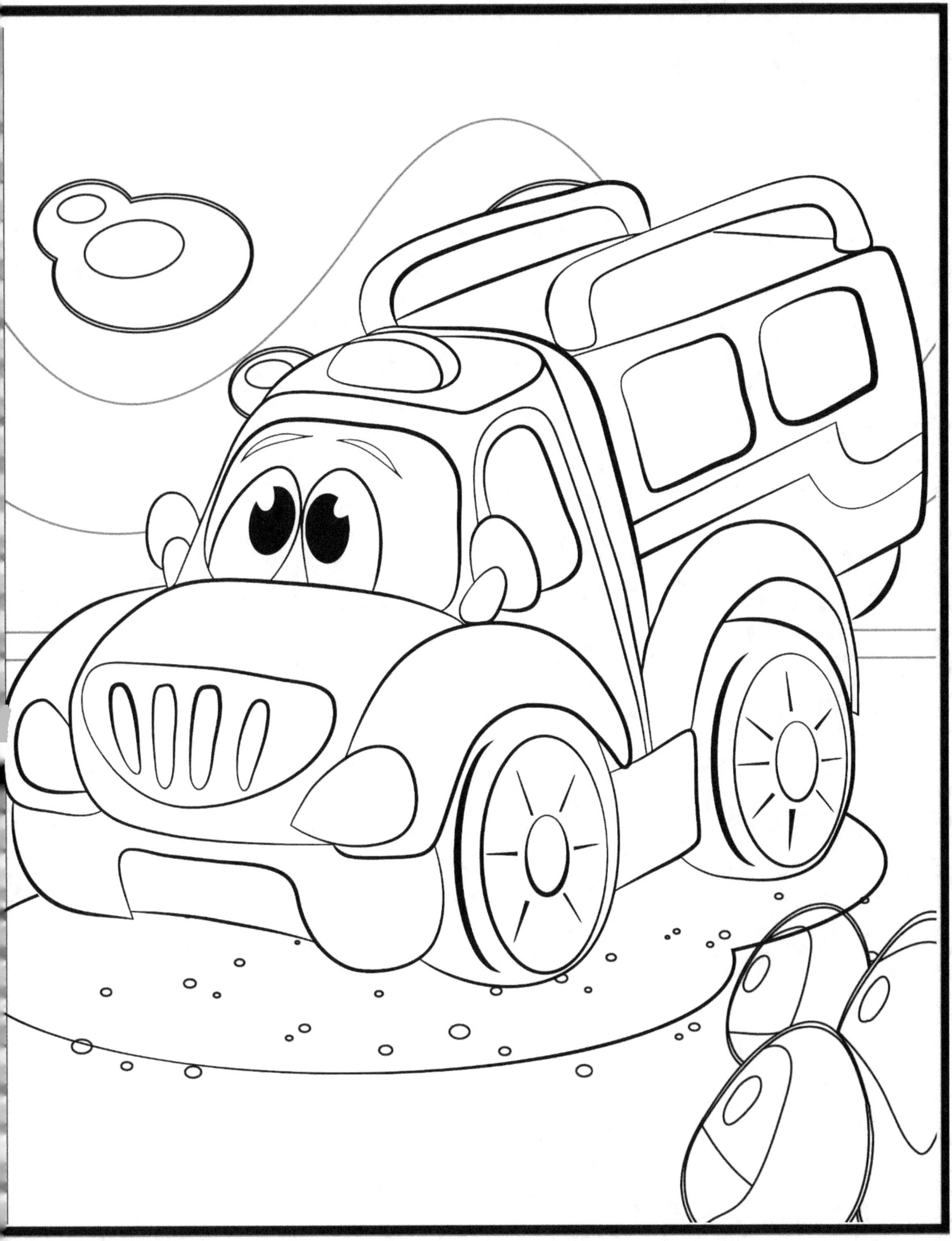

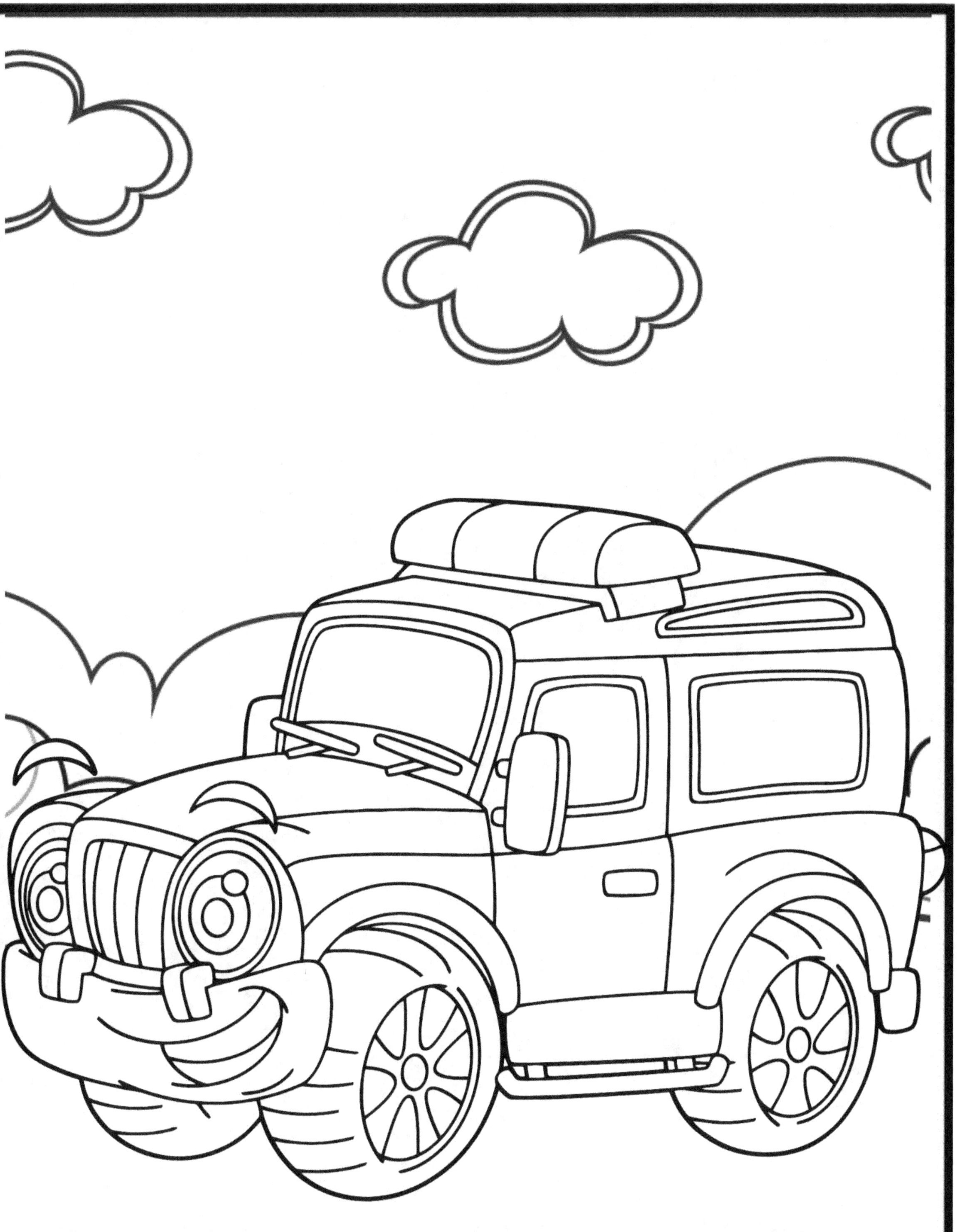

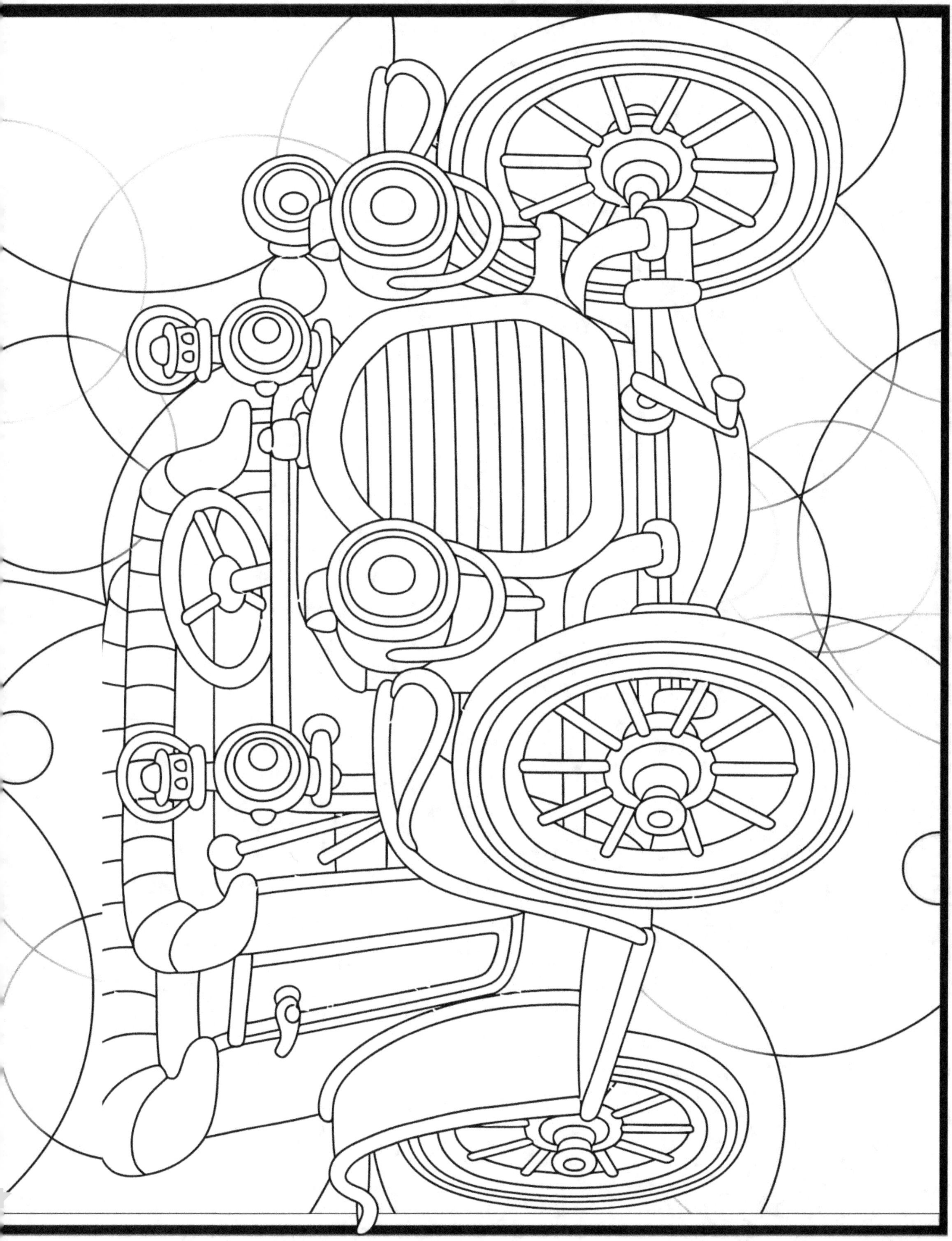

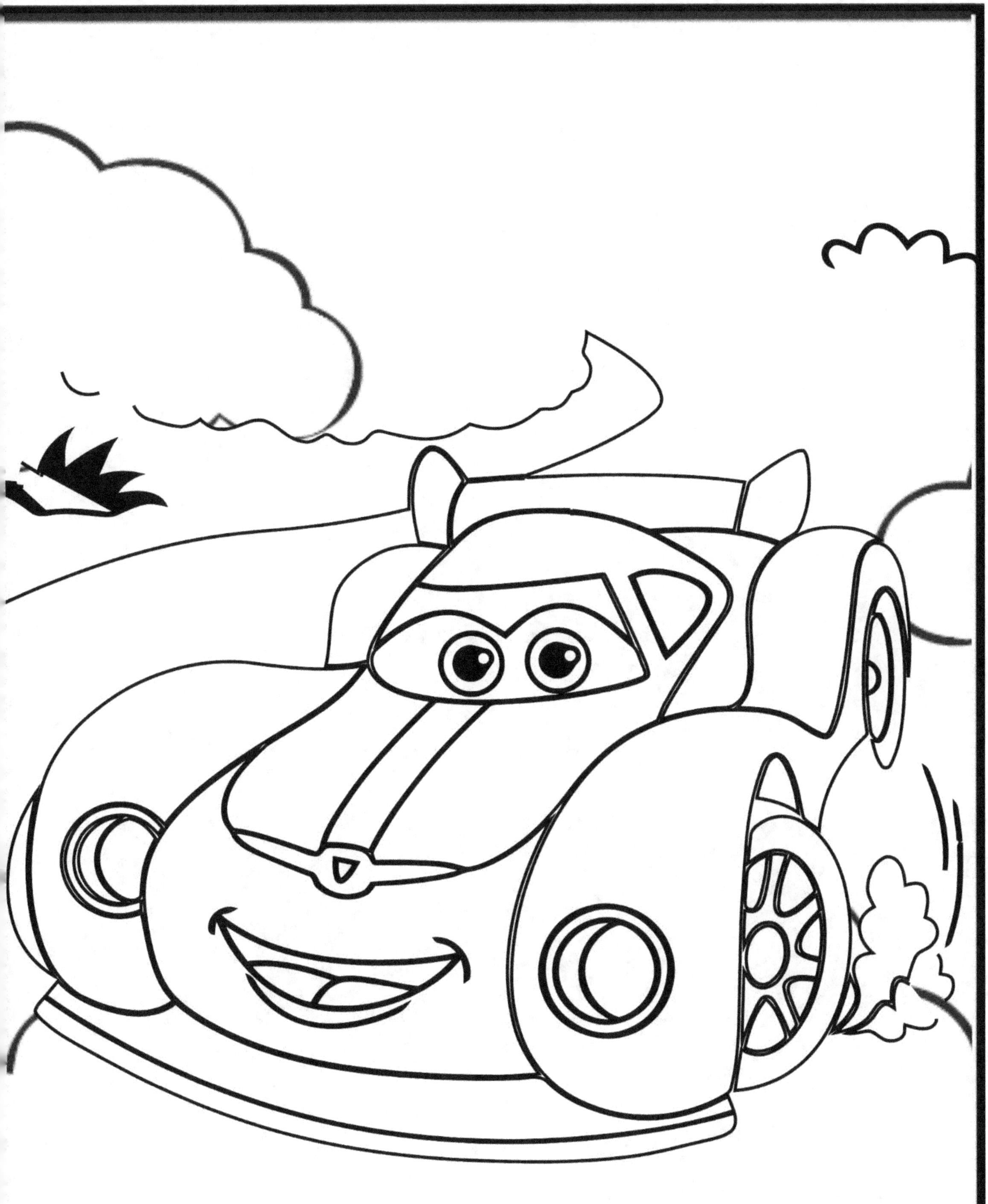

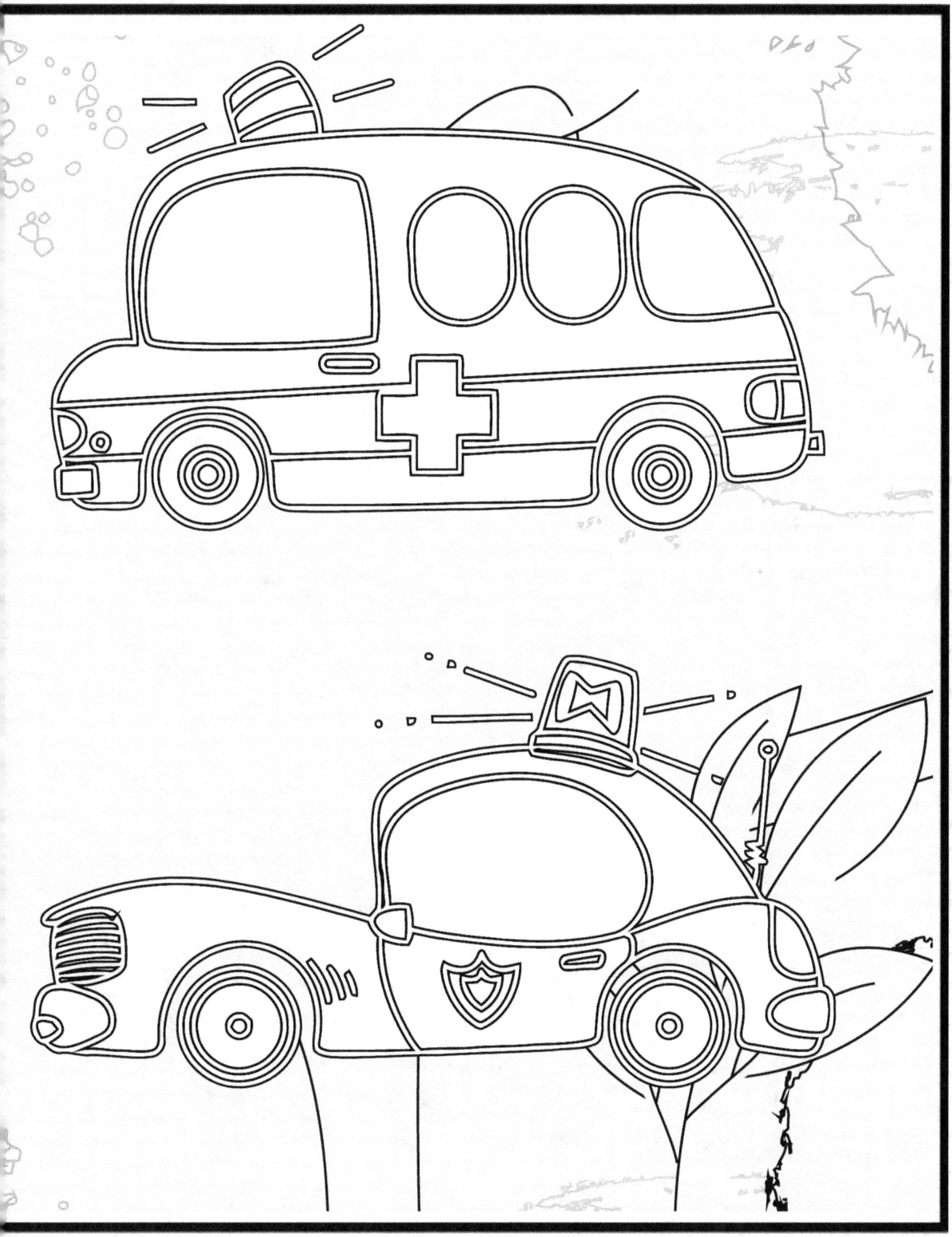

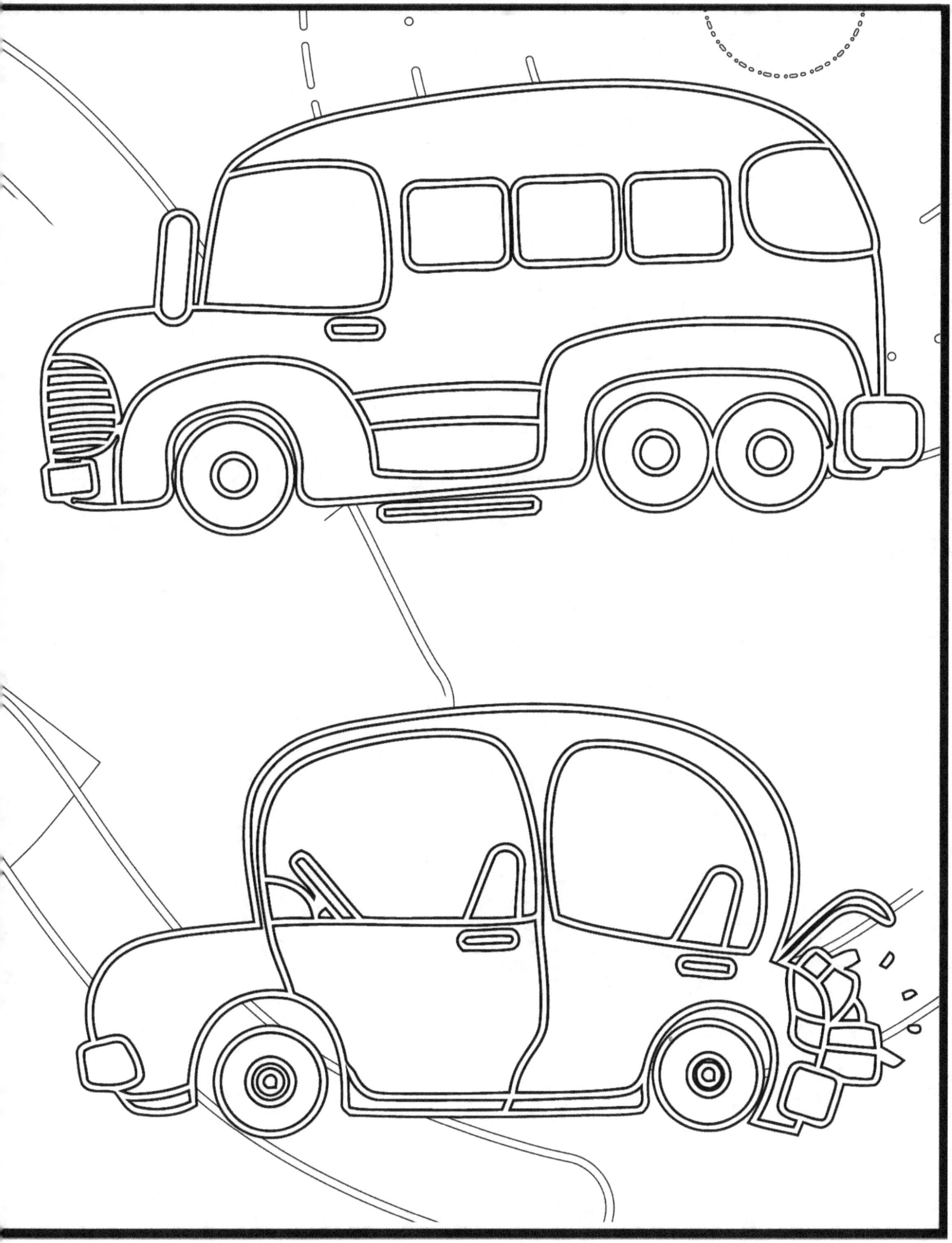

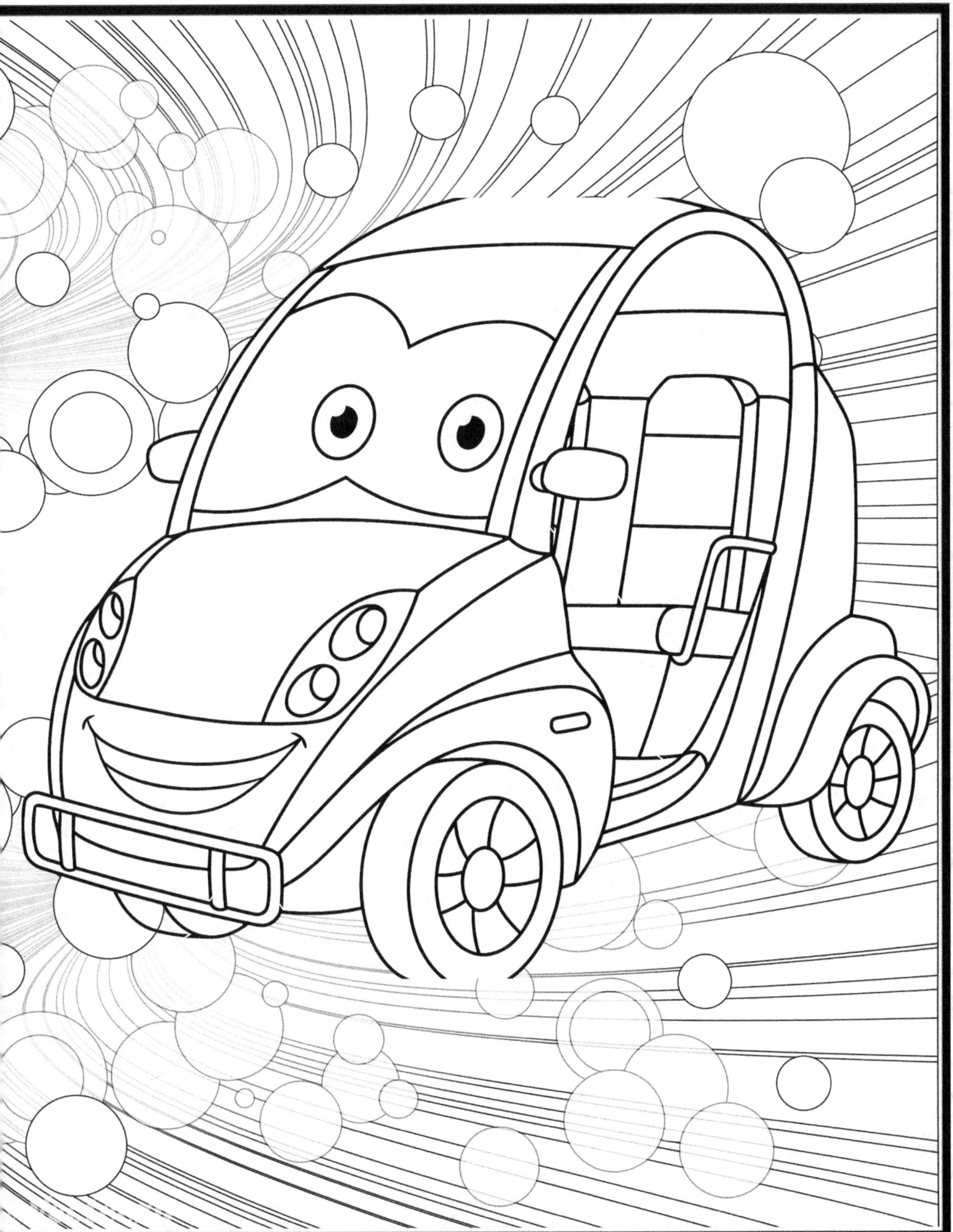

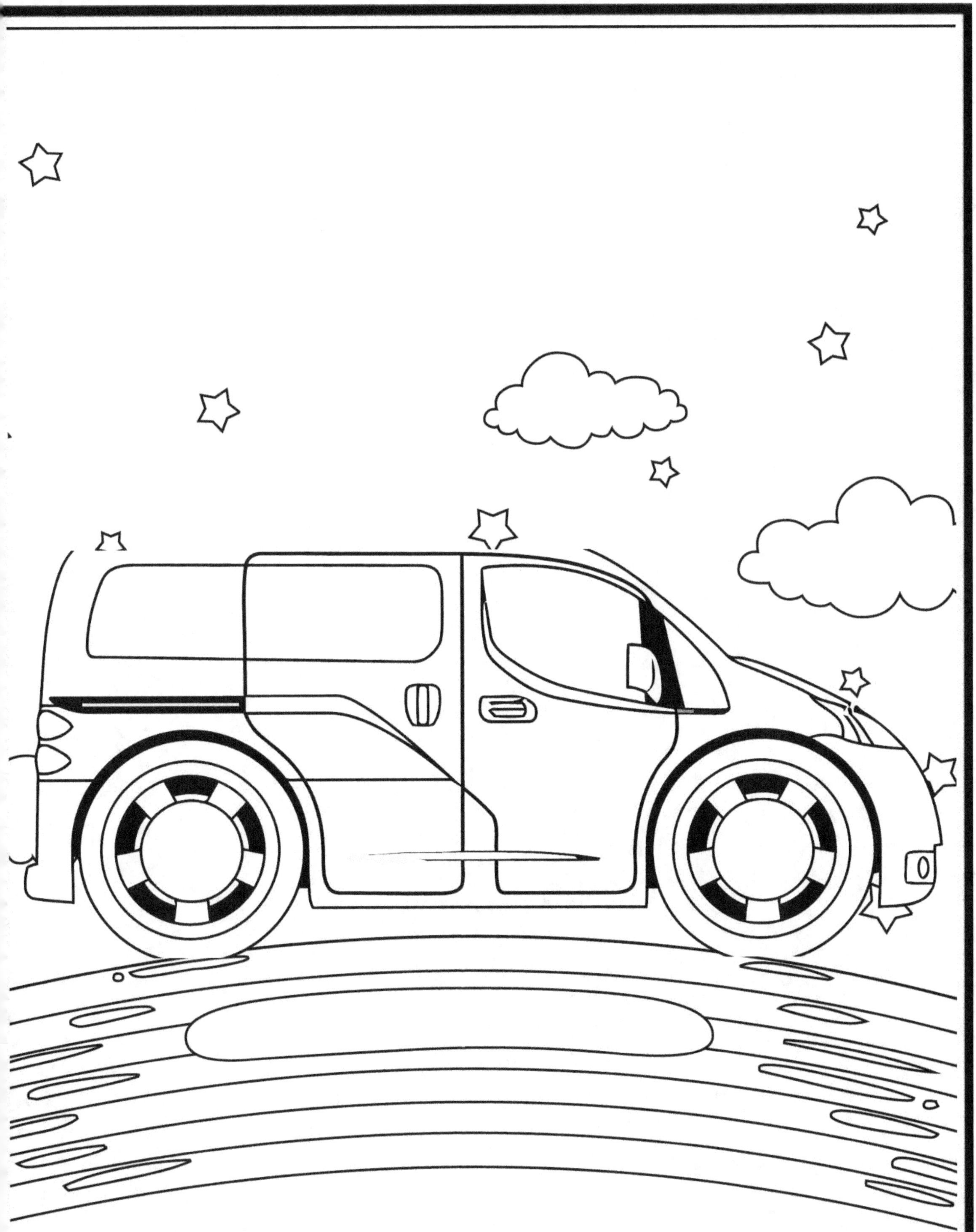

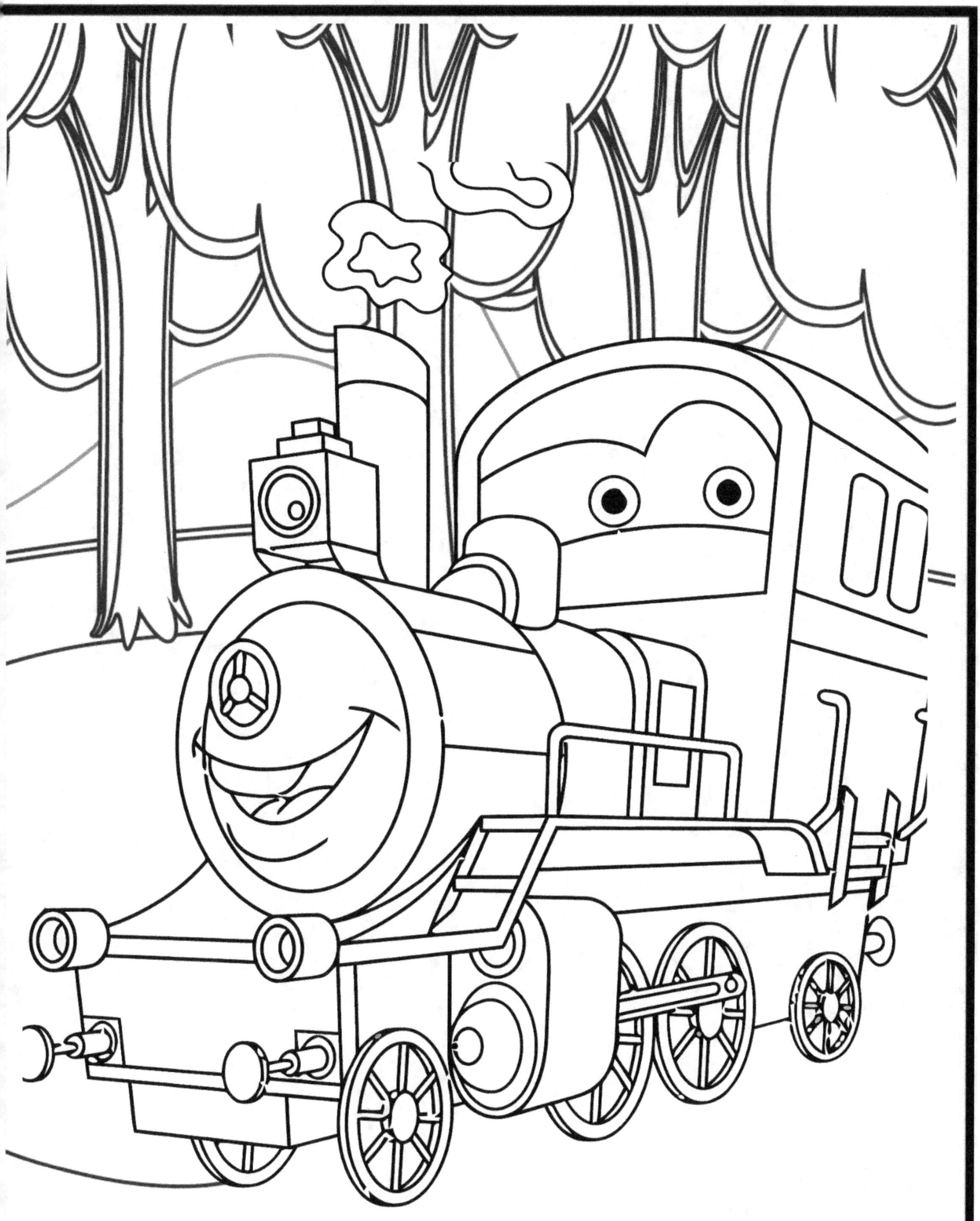

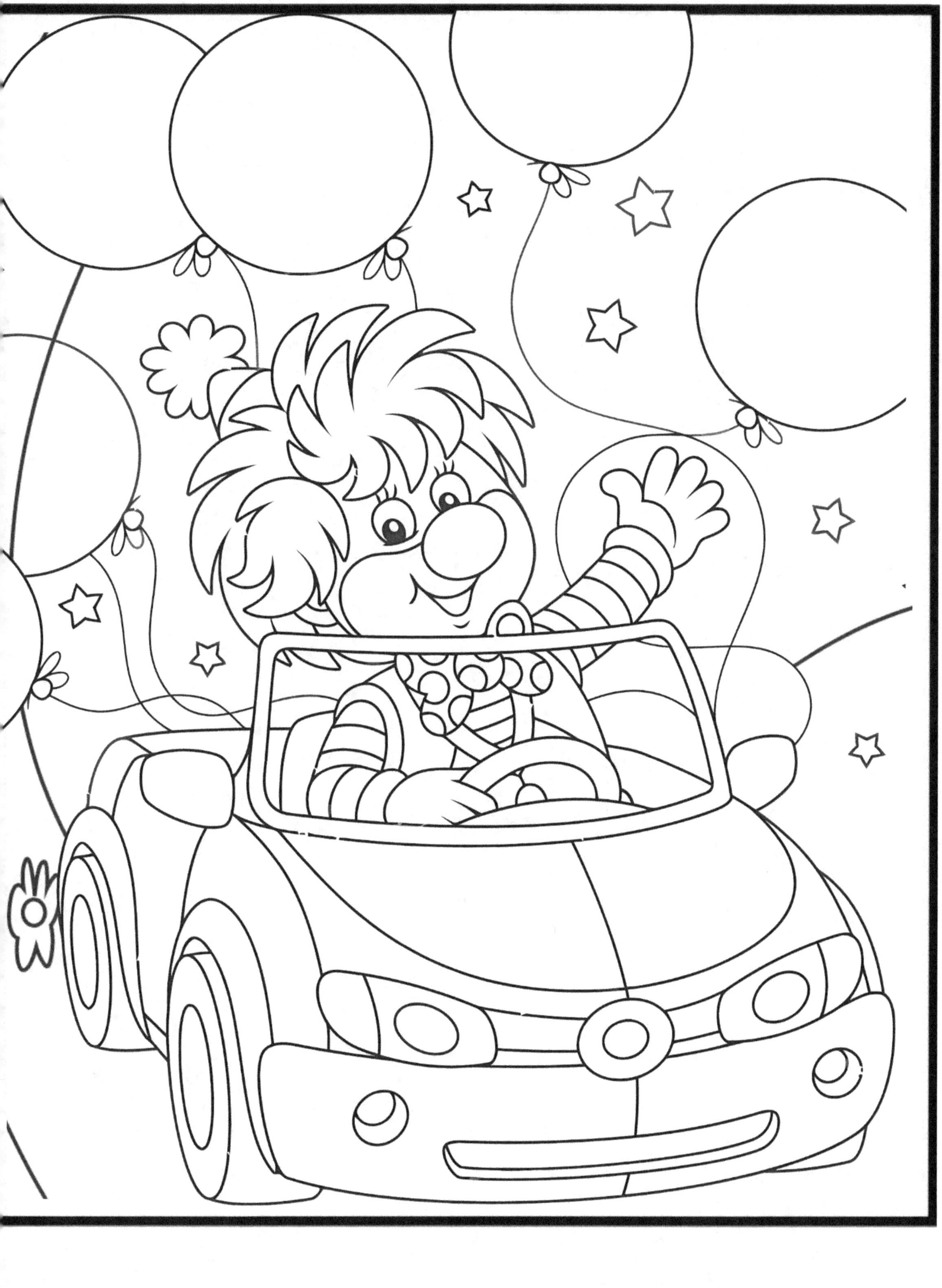

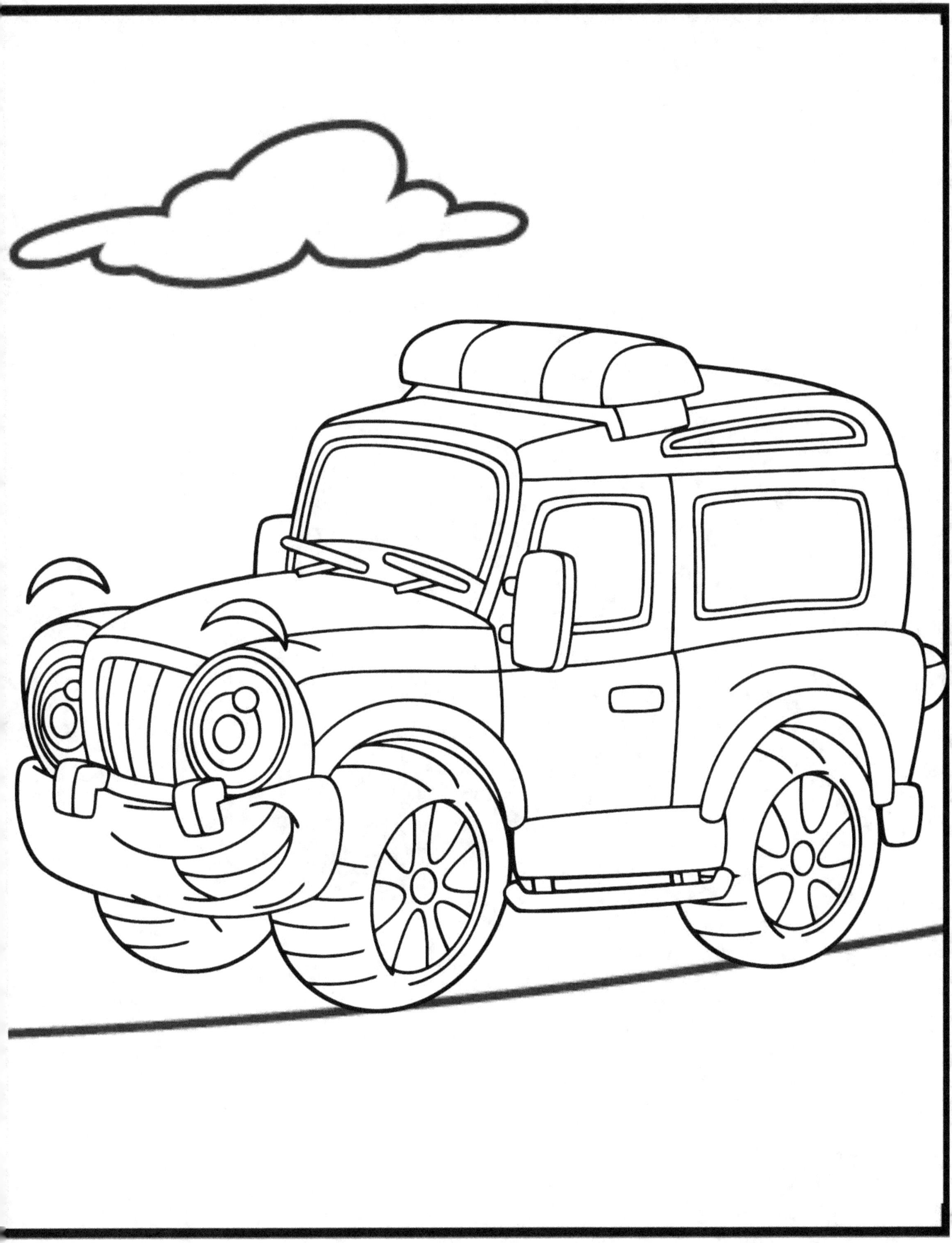

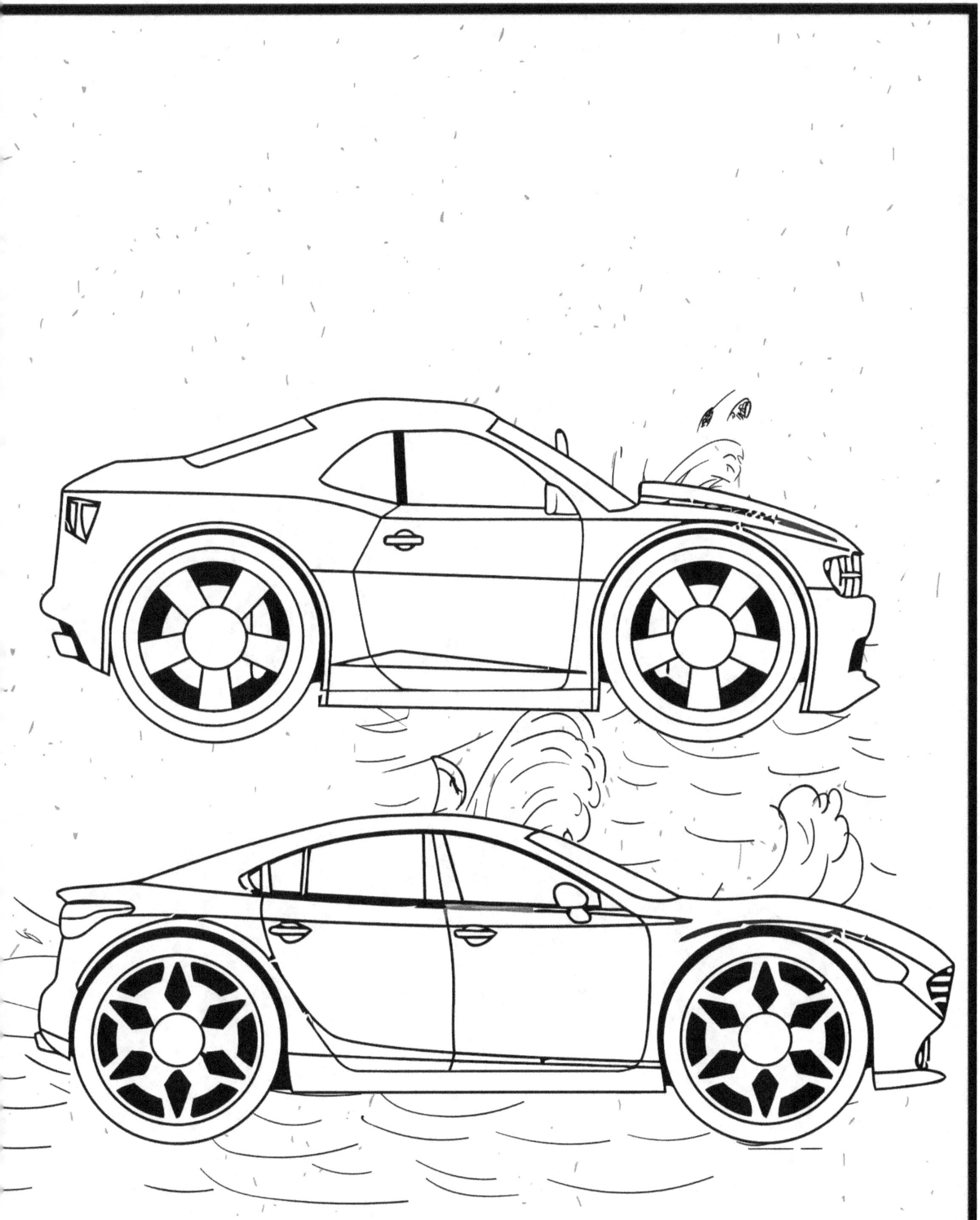

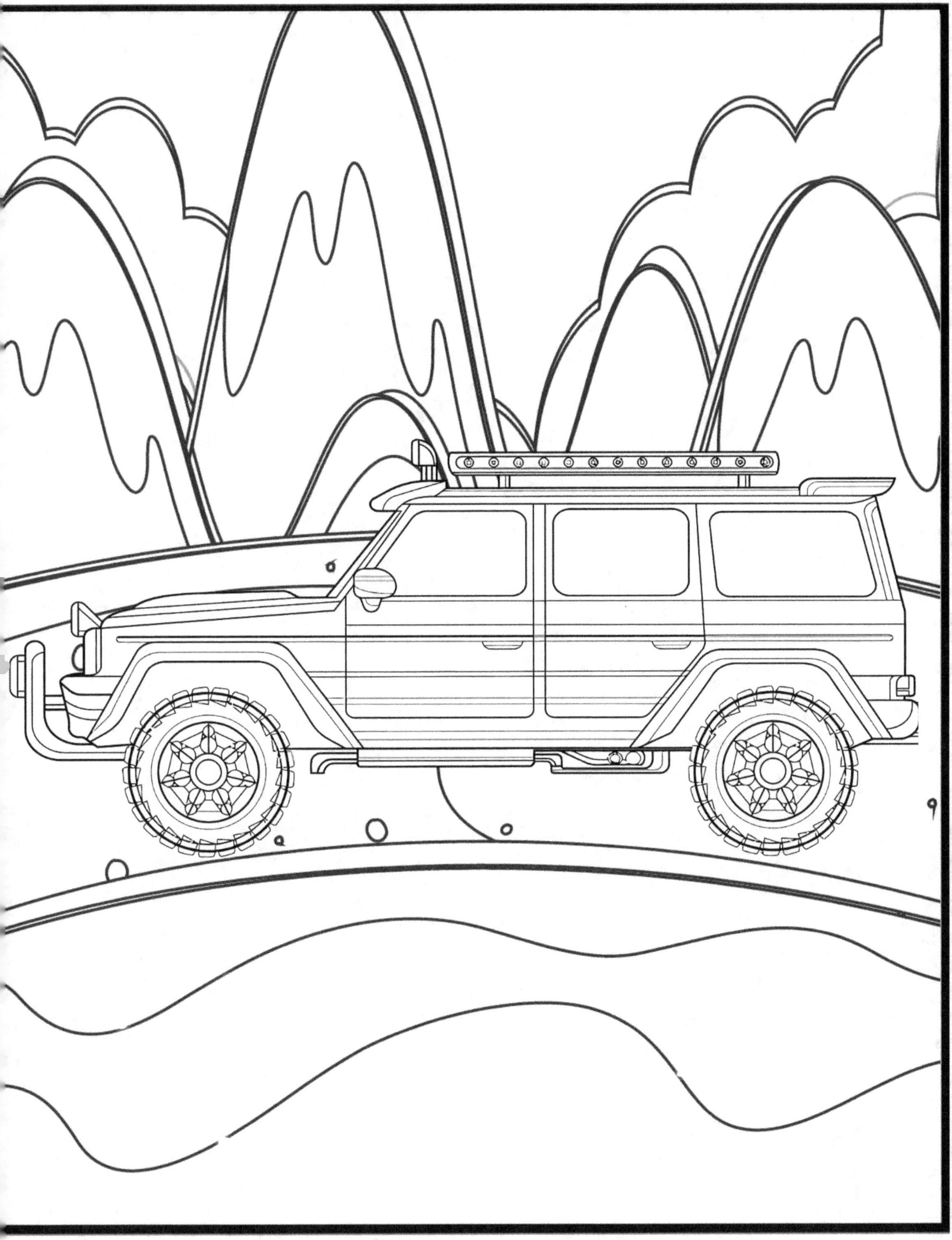

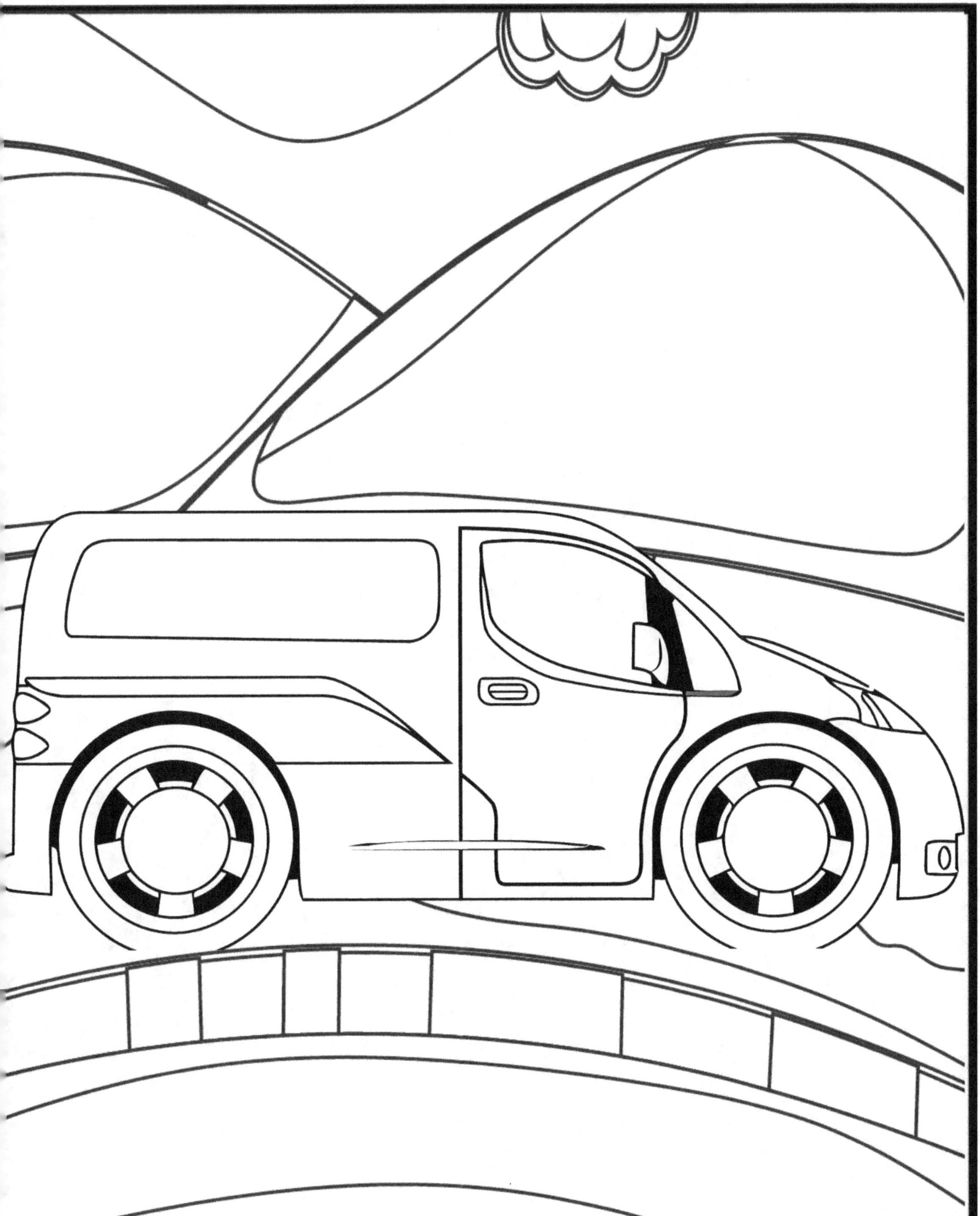

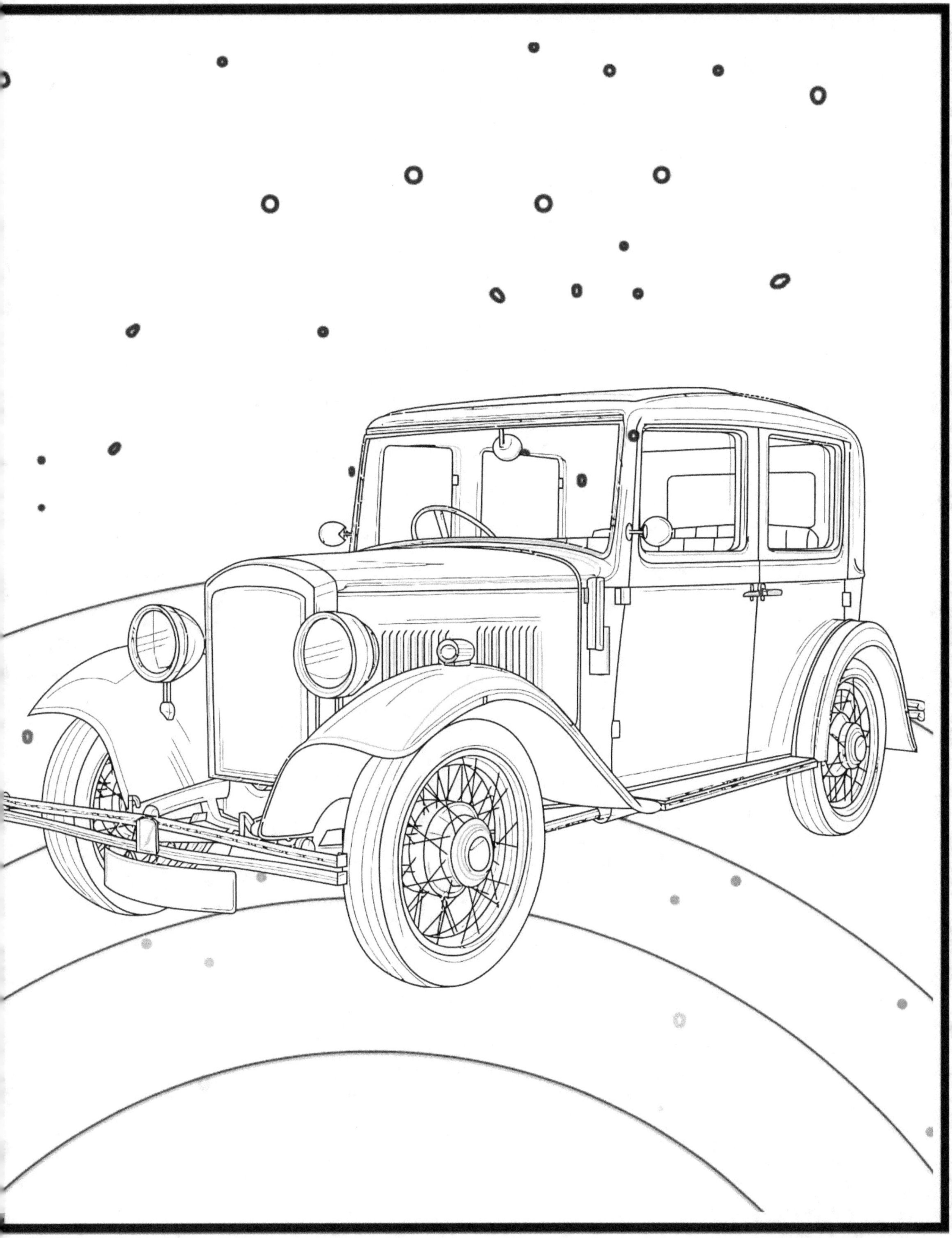

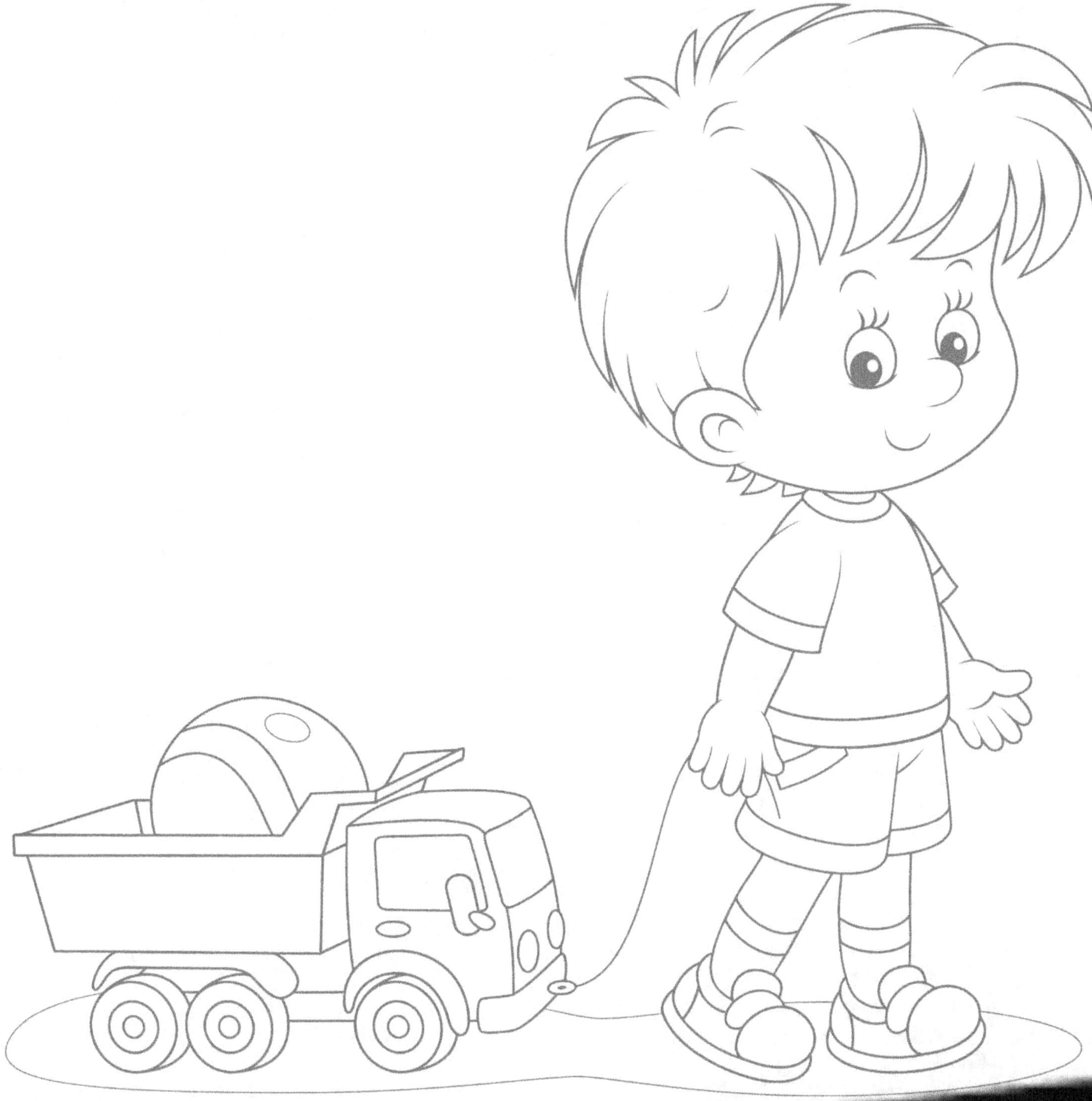

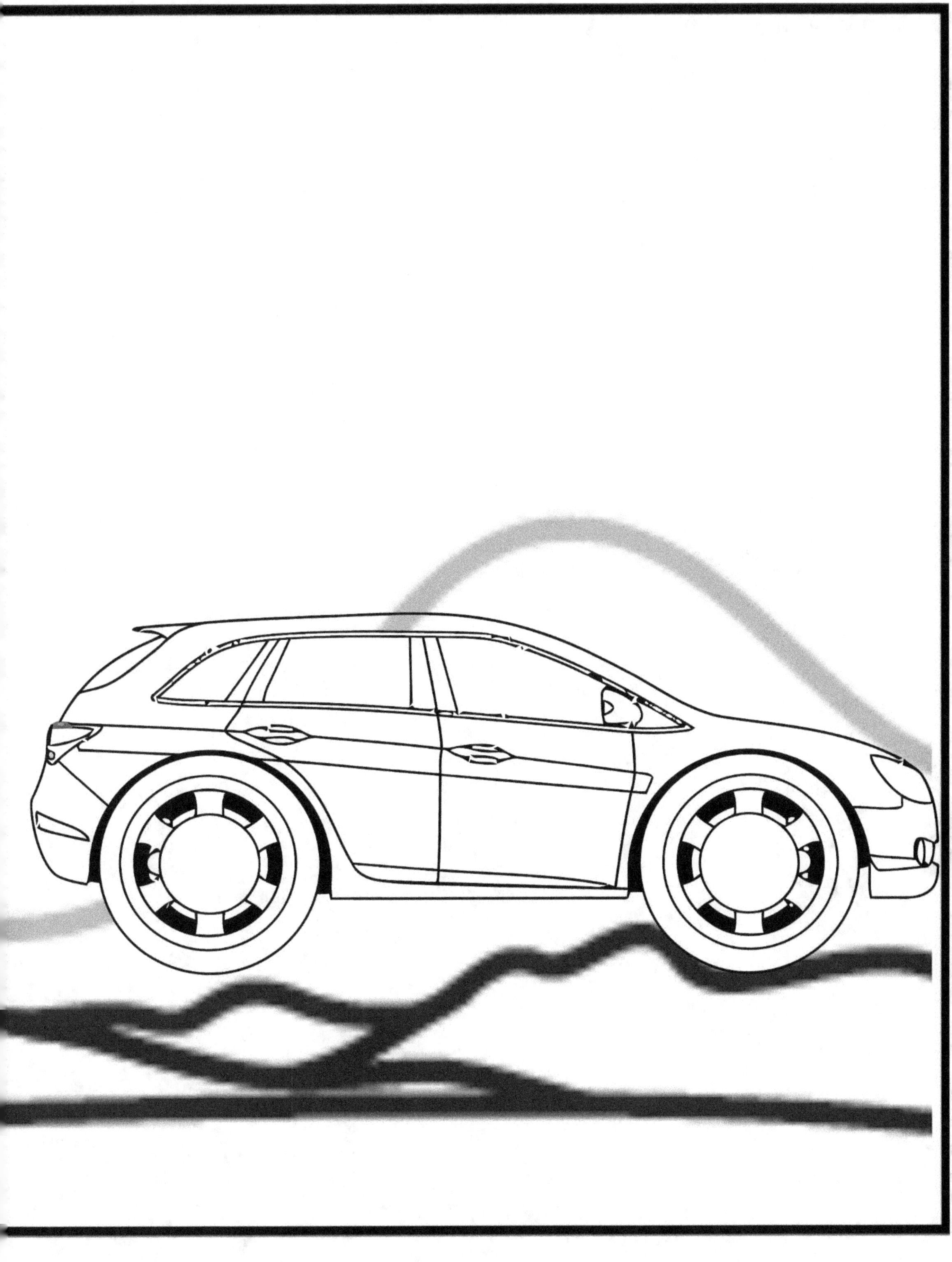

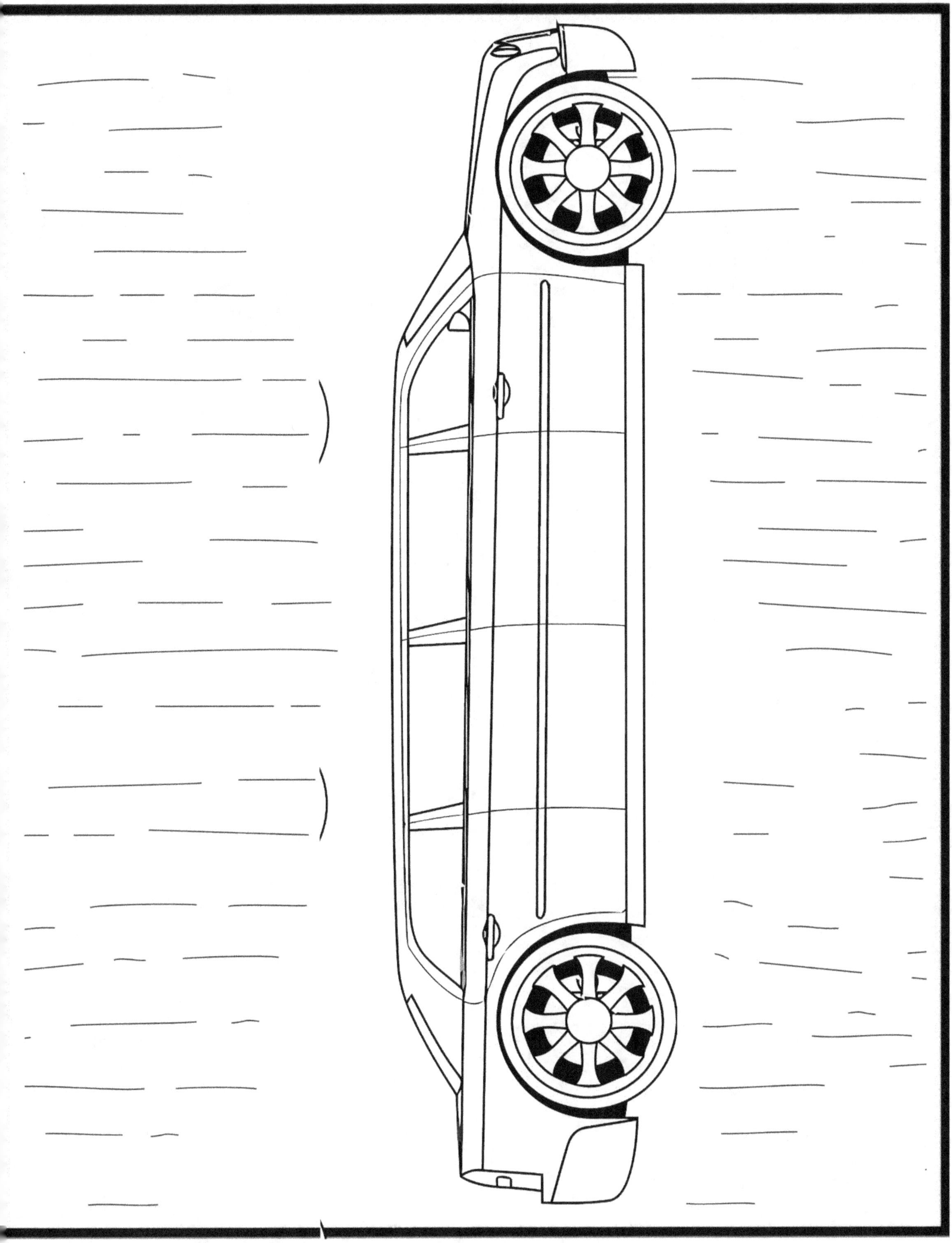

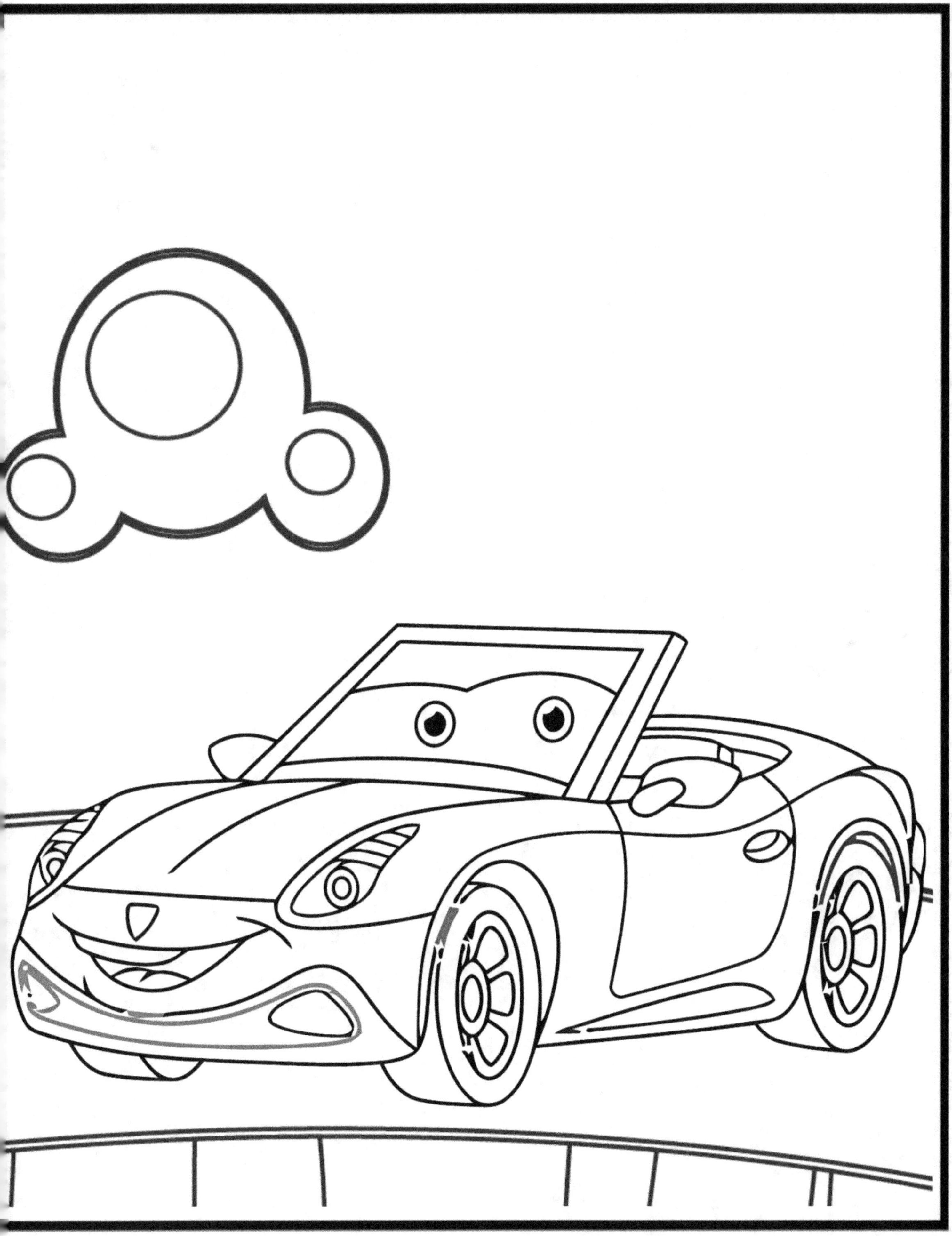

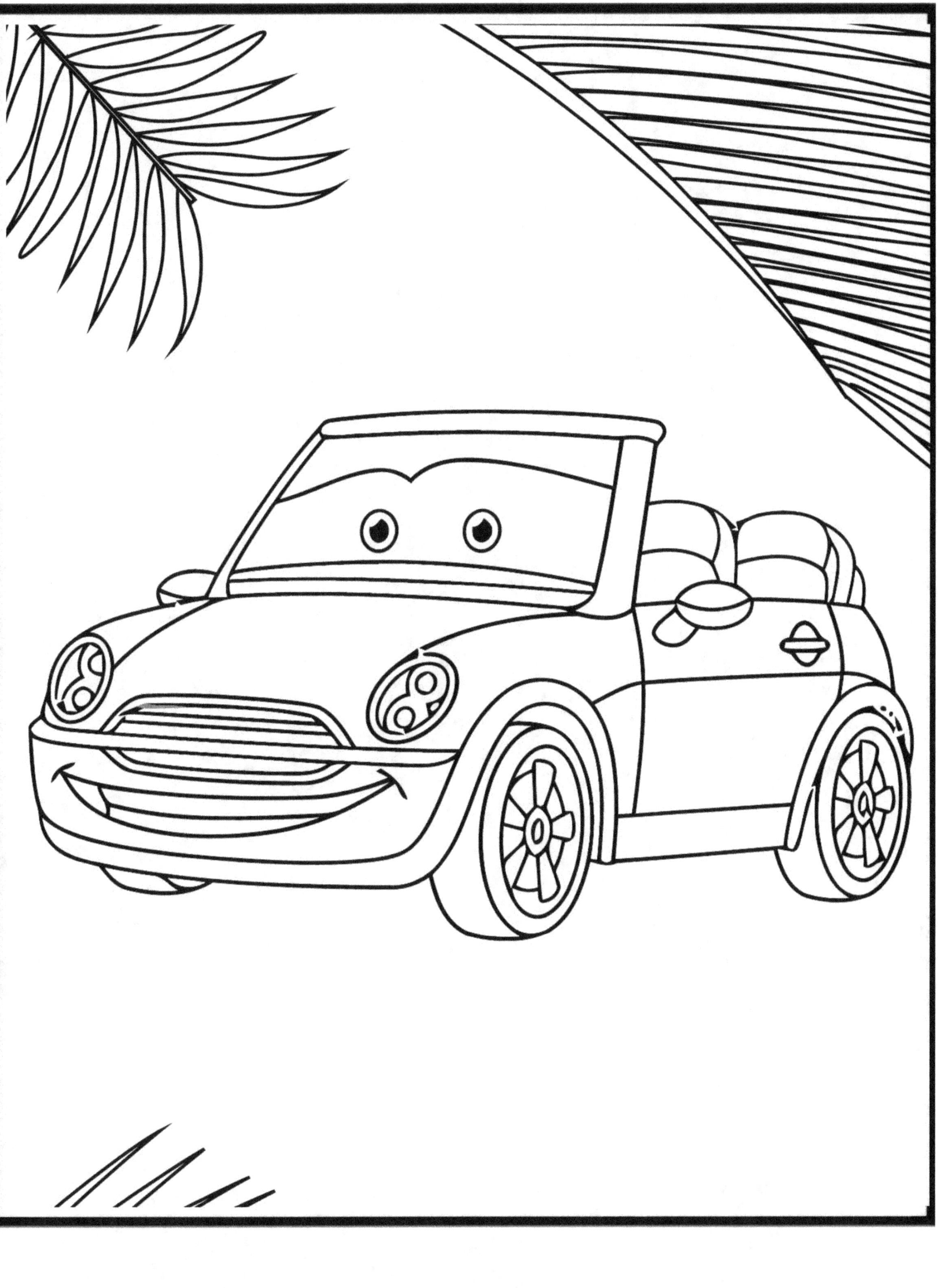

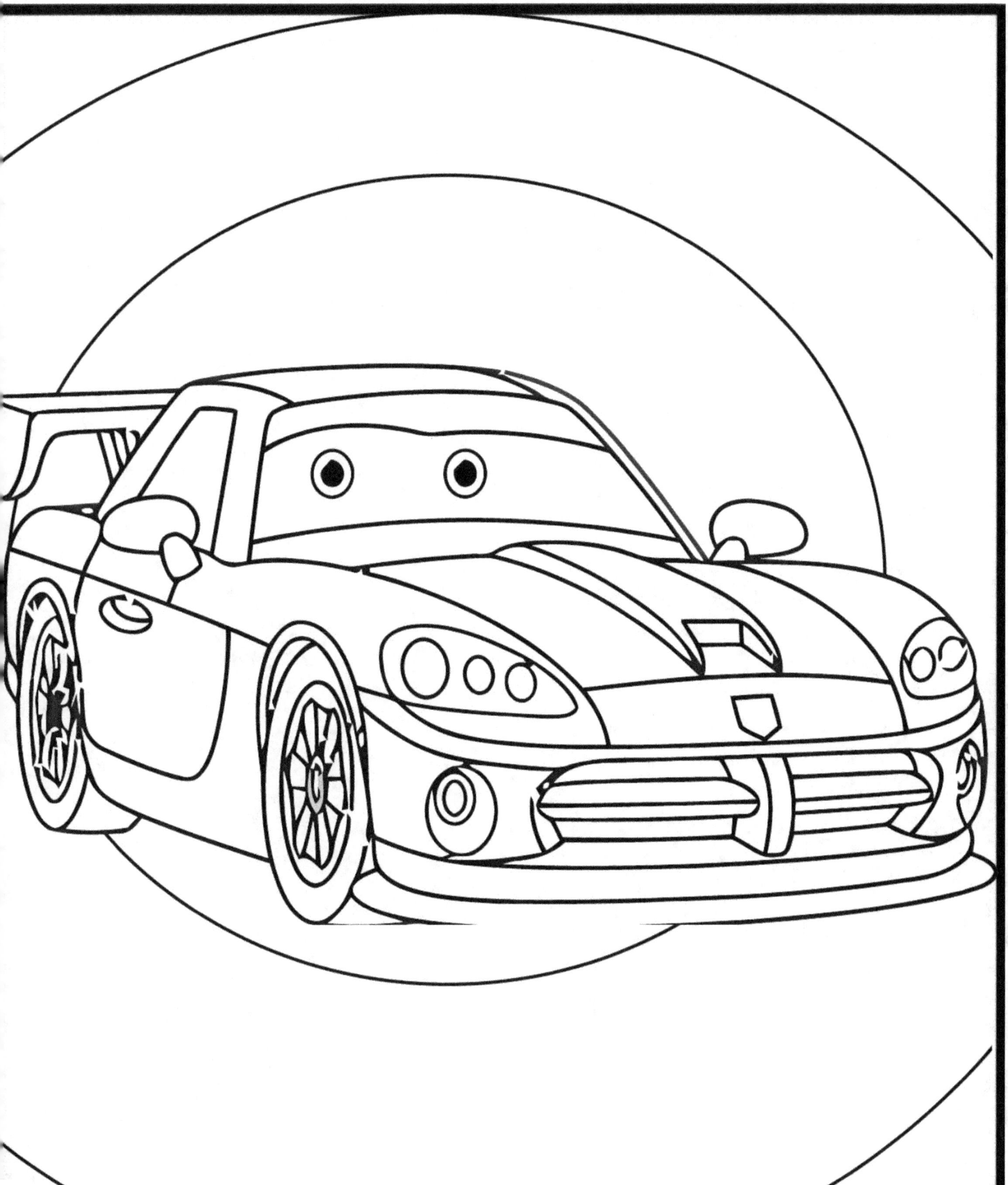

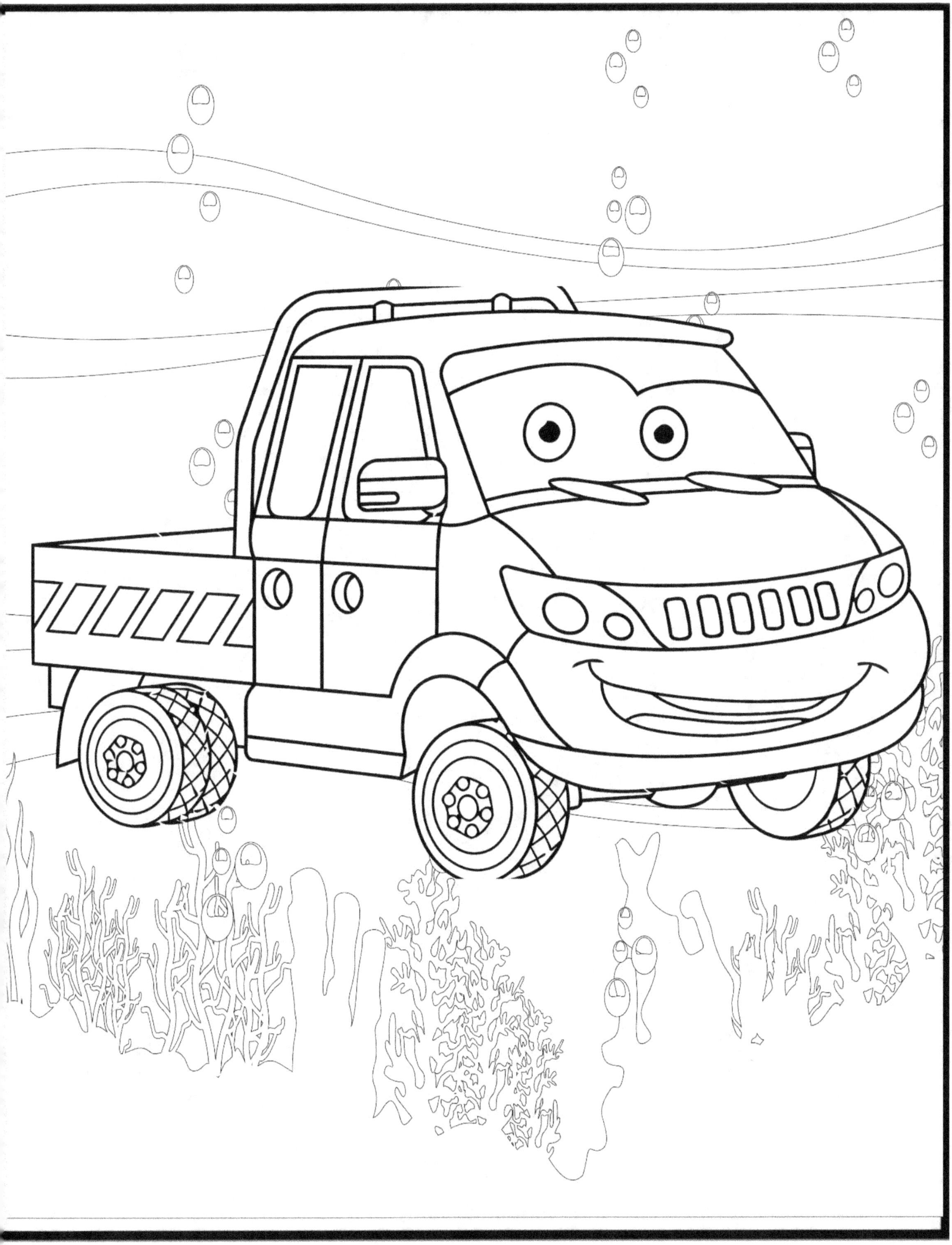

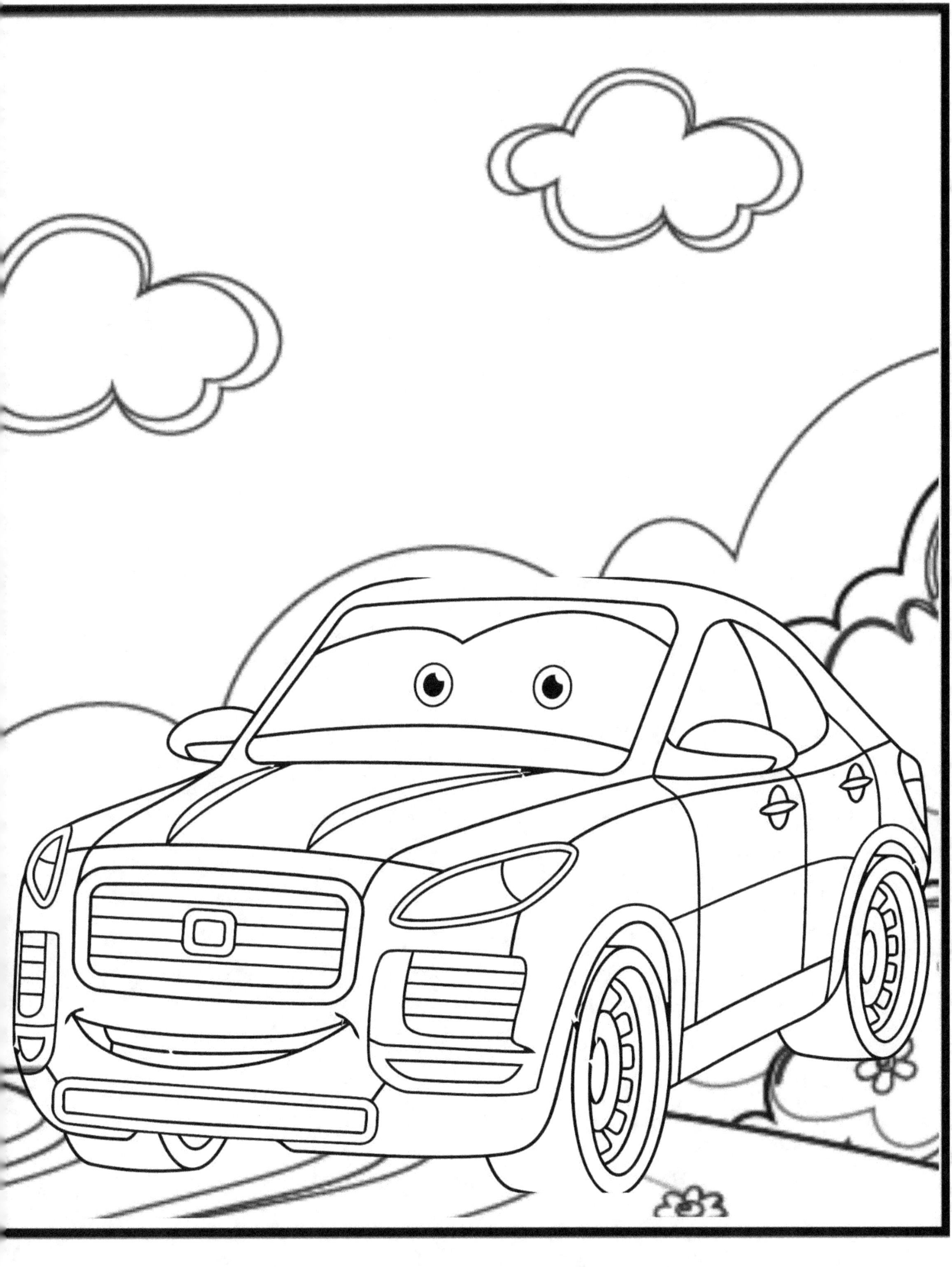

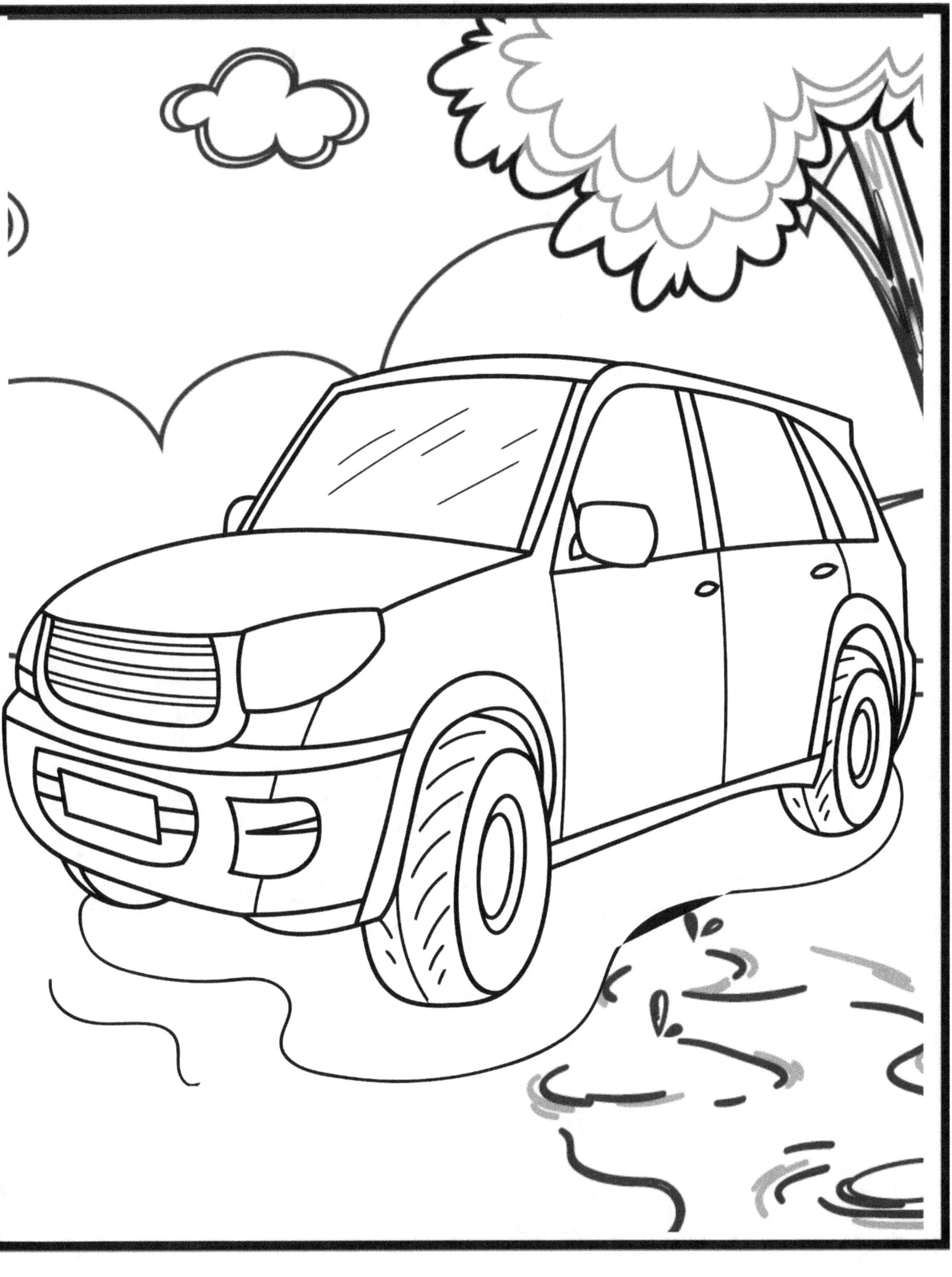

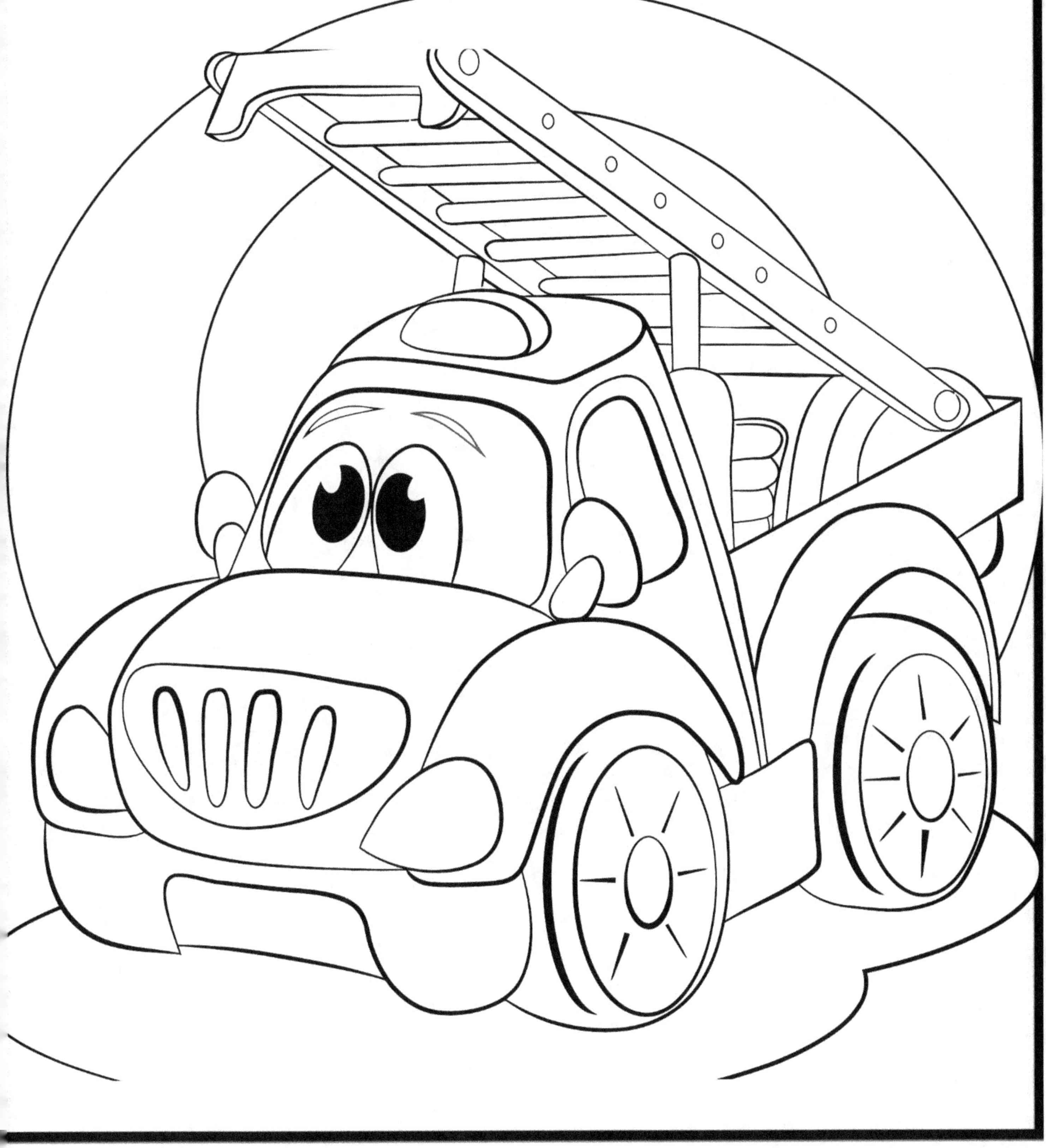

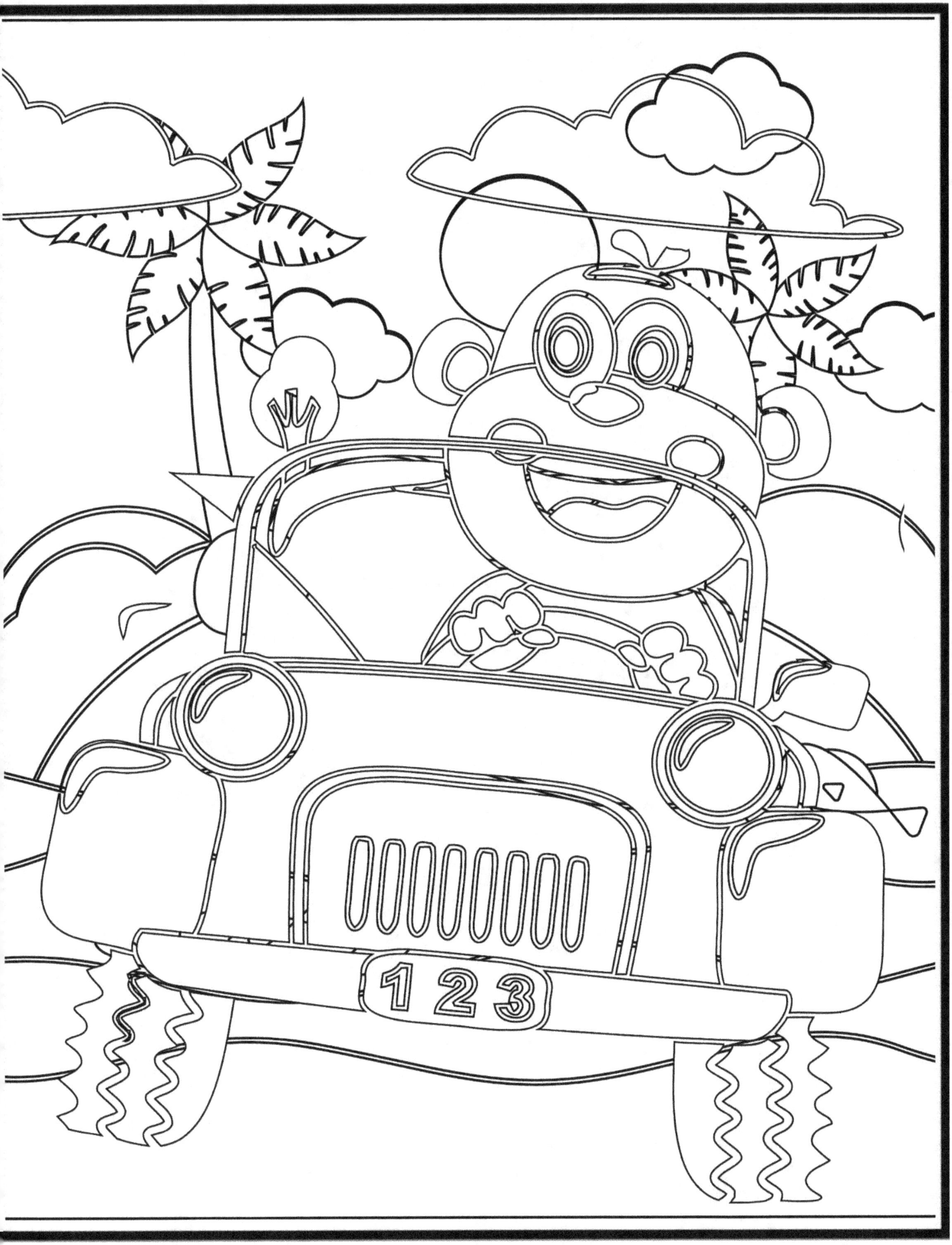
1 2 3

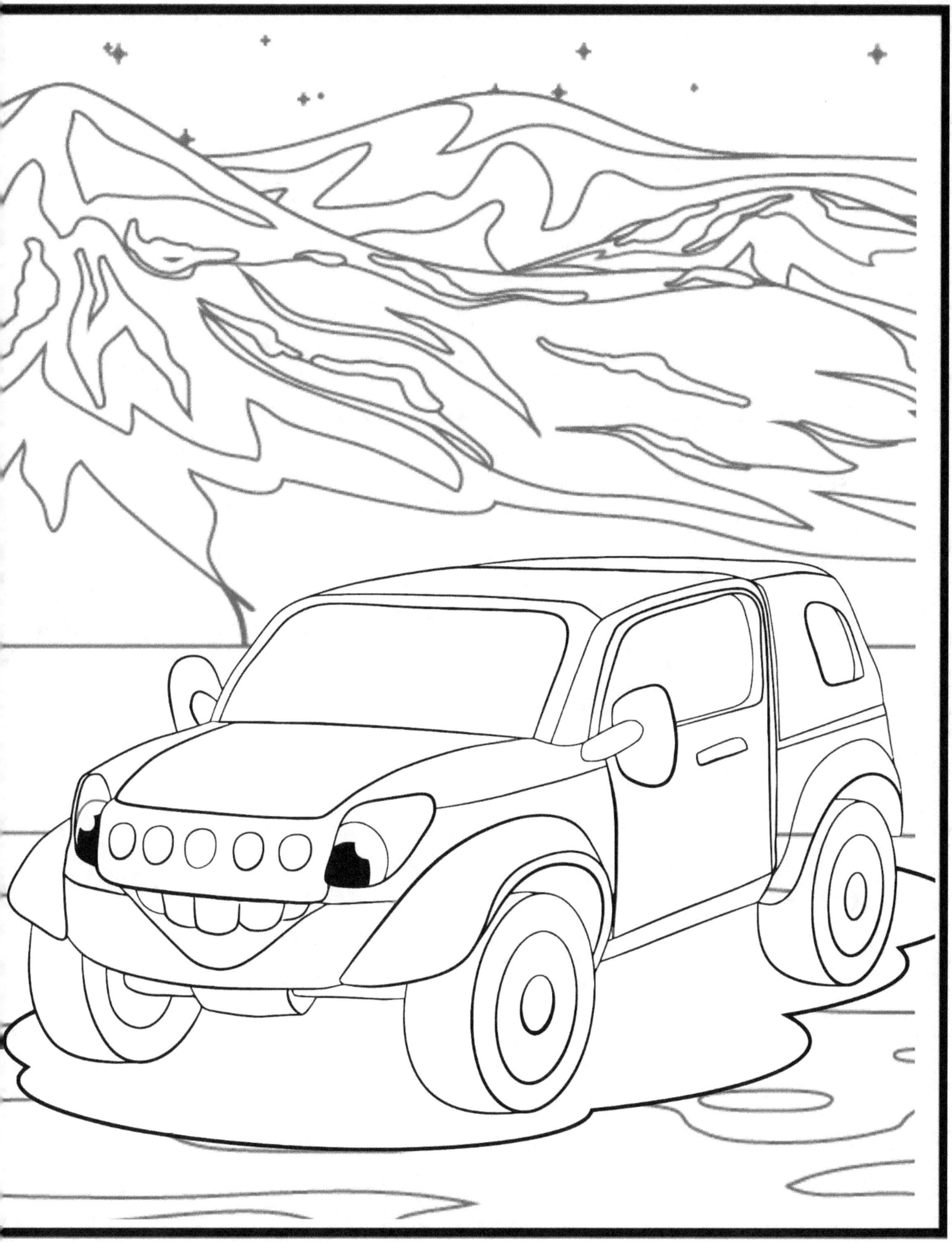

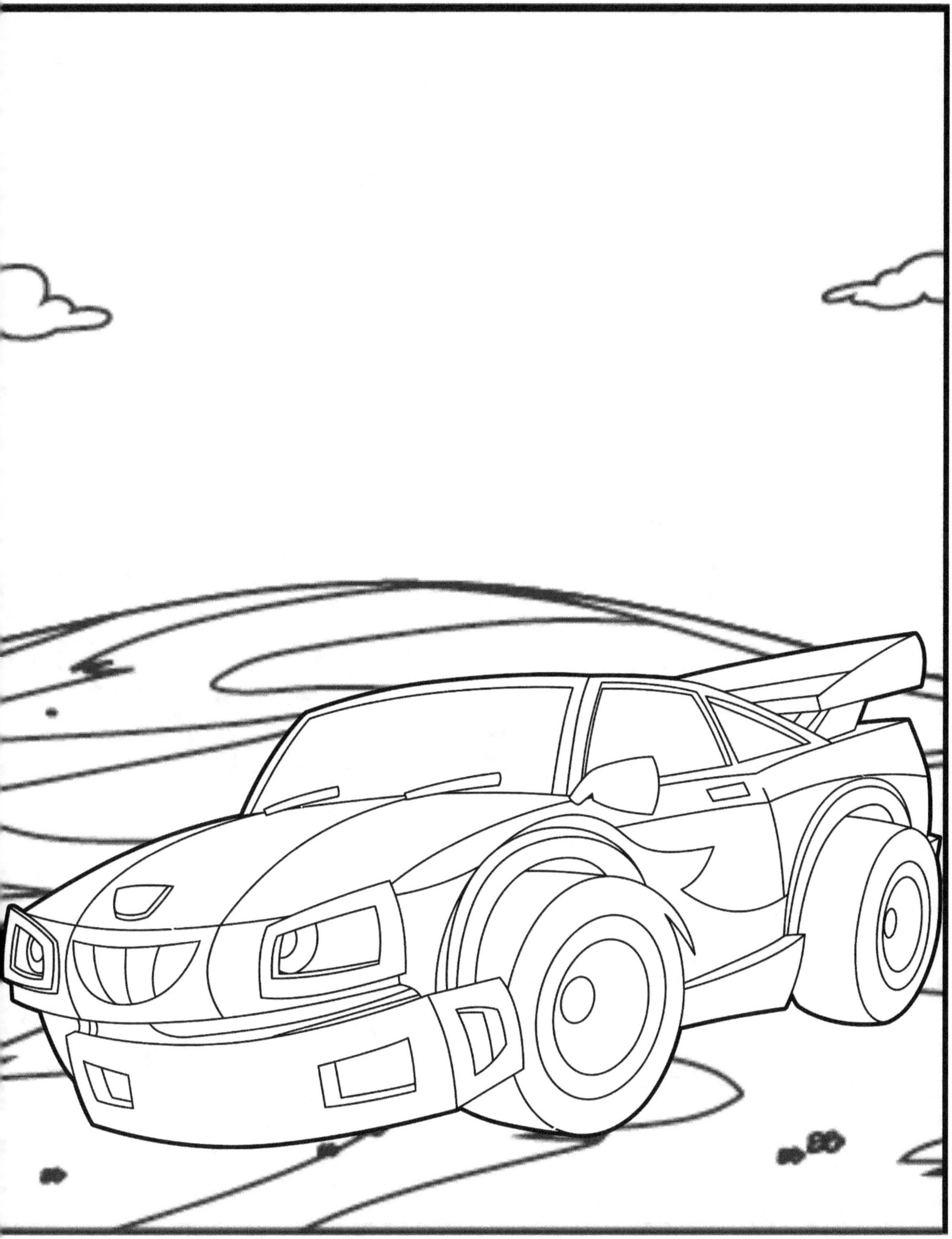

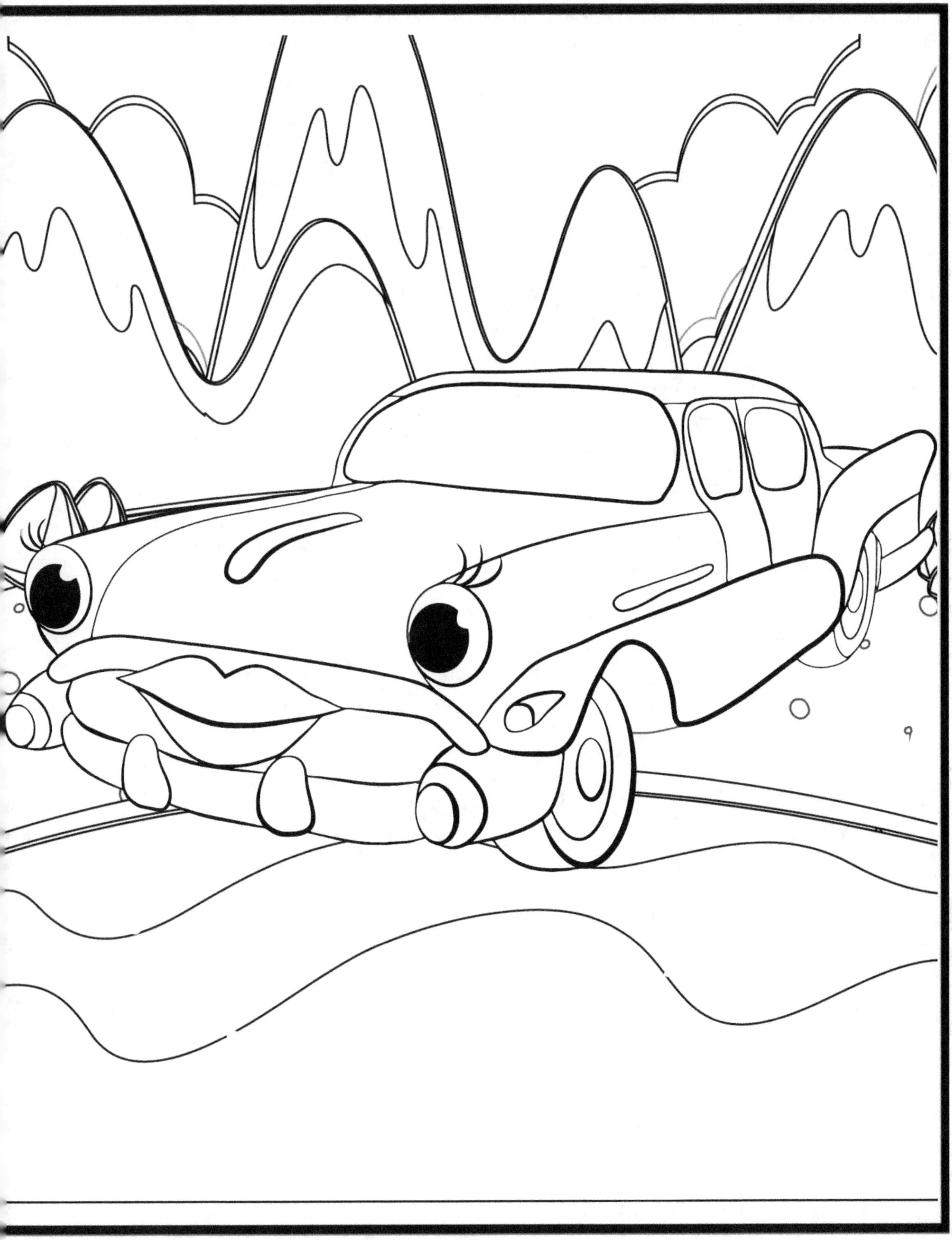

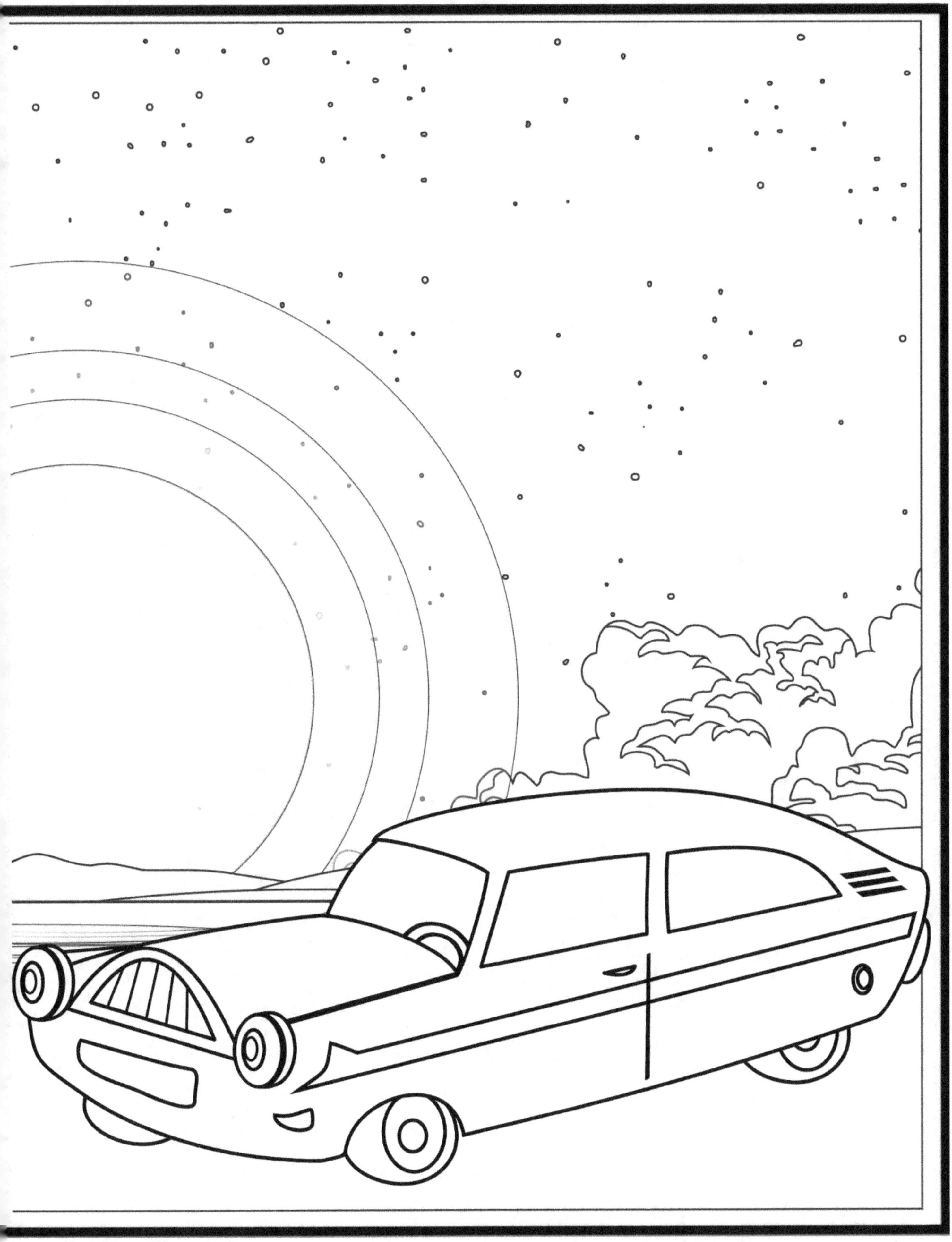

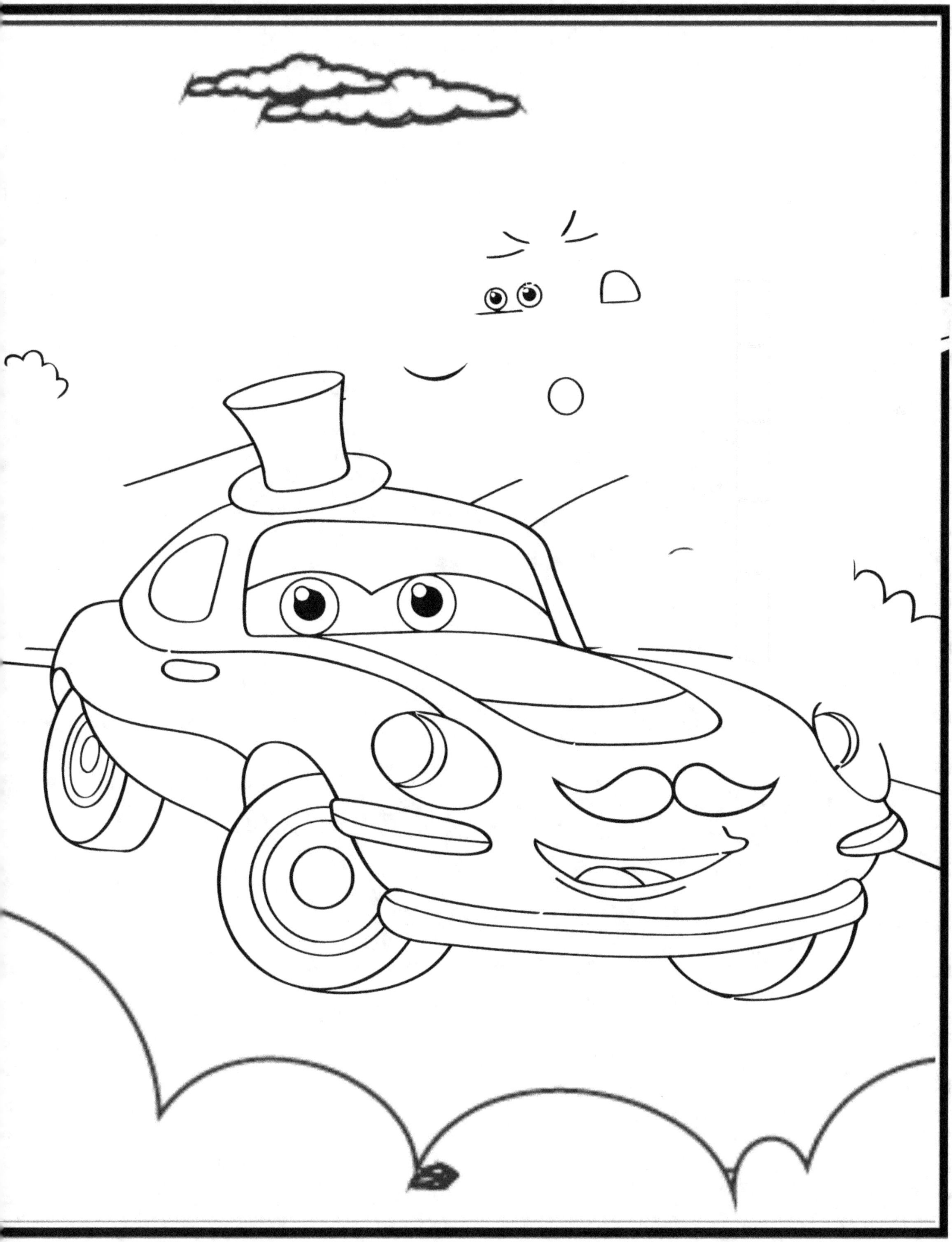

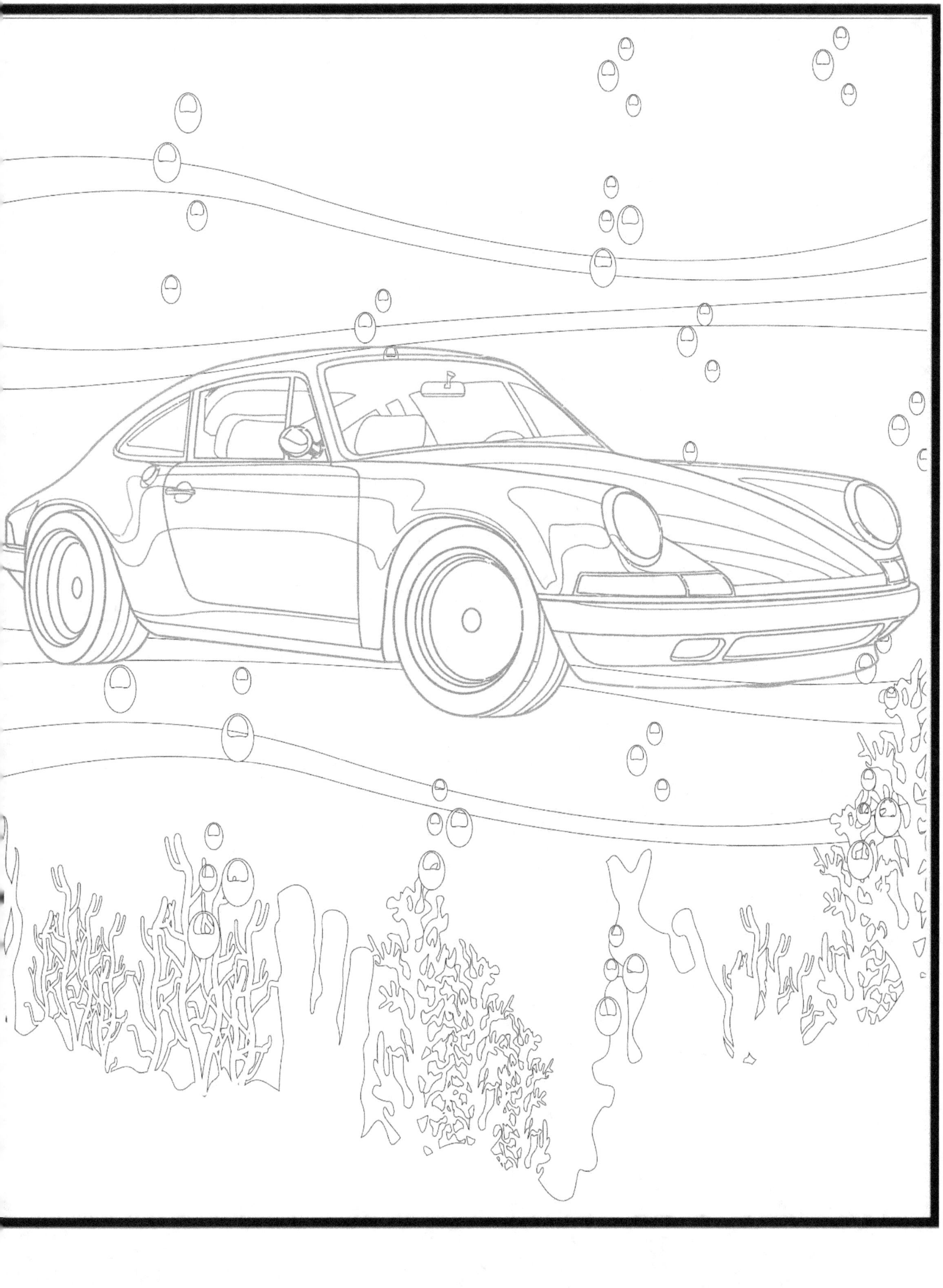

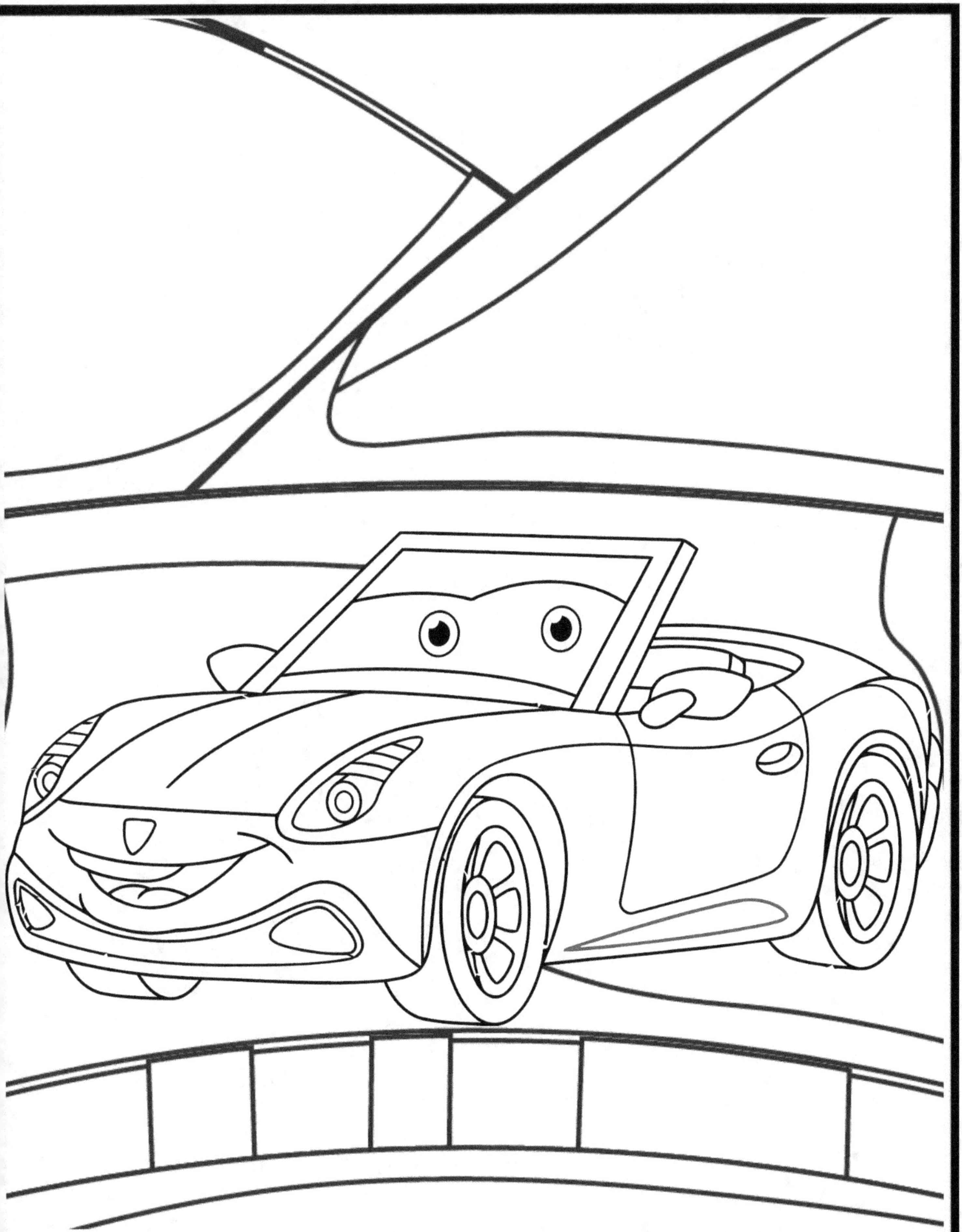

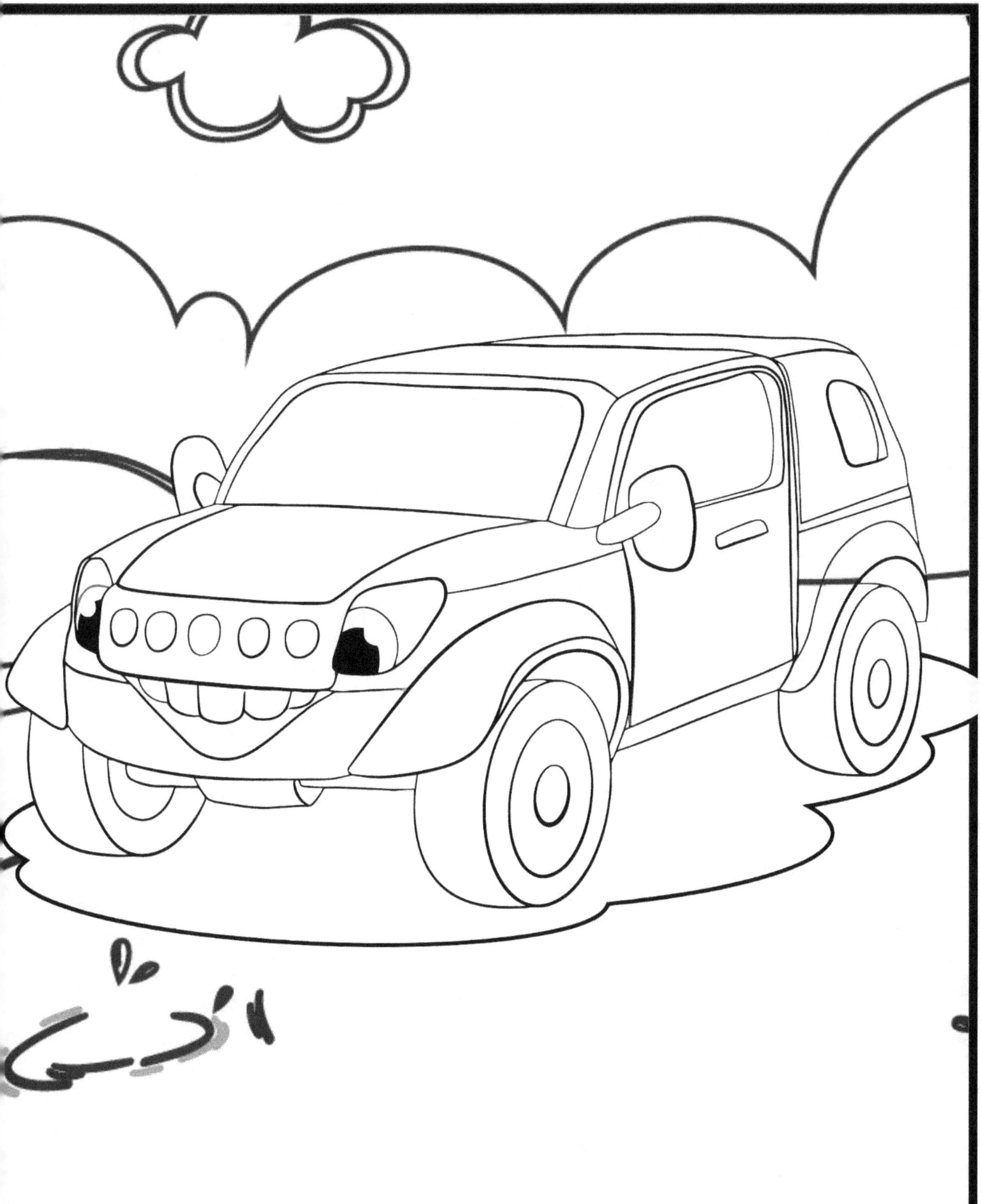

www.ingramcontent.com/pod-product-compliance
Lightning Source LLC
Chambersburg PA
CBHW080522220526
45465CB00006B/2564
9798749735062